Nomadic Soul

My Journey from the Libyan Sahara to a Jewish Life in Los Angeles

a memoir by

Ed Elhaderi

with Tom Fields-Meyer

LUMINARE PRESS

WWW.LUMINAREPRESS.COM

Nomadic Soul
My Journey from the Libyan Sahara to a Jewish Life in Los Angeles
© 2019 Ed Elhaderi

Cover Artwork—Monoprint by Barbara Elhaderi
Cover Design and Book Layout by Claire Flint Last
Map Artwork by Barbara Elhaderi
Author Photo taken by Barbara Elhaderi

Luminare Press
438 Charnelton St., Suite 101
Eugene, OR 97401
www.luminarepress.com

ISBN: 978-1-944733-82-7
LOC: 2018964648

This book is dedicated to my family.

*To the memory of my maternal grandmother, Jida Gazalla,
who gave me guidance and a foundation of love that
sustained me during my formative years.*

*With love and admiration for my wife, Barbara,
my daughter, Jessica, and my son, Jason,
who, individually and collectively, have assisted me
and encouraged me to seek my true inner self.*

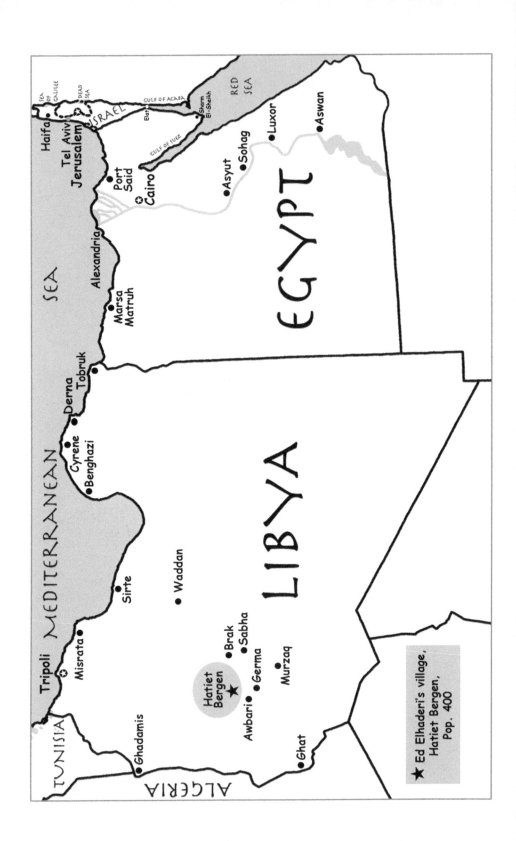

TABLE OF CONTENTS

Foreword

As I read Ed Elhaderi's memoir, I kept hearing the words God said to Abram (later called Abraham), our Biblical father: *Lech lecha,* "Go forth from your land, the land of your birth, the house of your father to the land that I will show you." A Hasidic master pointed out that the phrase *lech lecha,* ordinarily translated as "go forth," has a more literal meaning: *lech* means to go or walk, and *lecha,* "unto yourself" or "for yourself."

In retrospect, Ed's journey outward is also a journey inward. It is not only a process of discovering a new land and language, a new world and people, a new sense of inner tranquility and direction. It is also an inner journey of discovering how to stitch together the world from which he came—the rural, primitive, poor village in Libya of the 1950s and early 1960s—and the world in which he lives, as a Jew-by-choice in twenty-first-century Los Angeles.

I must confess that I thought I knew Ed. After all, we attend the same synagogue each week and greet each other as friends. He is always respectful and courteous, even a bit shy. One is mindful that he is not native born. His manners were shaped by a different culture, one more traditional than the avant-garde world of the city in which we live. But the more I read of his life, the more I understood that I had only glimpsed at the depth of his story, the length of his journey.

Ed grew up in a rural village in Libya, far removed from urban life—certainly the urban life of twenty-first-century Hollywood. He was raised with little contact with the outside world, no television, and limited access to radio, occasional newspapers, and few books. His world was oral—words that were spoken, stories that were told. And yet he is able to convey that world, to depict his distant father and his loving mother, his extended family and his brother, the friends that shaped him, and the restrictions of that world.

Education offered him an opportunity, his intellect taking him from his village to the big city, and, ultimately, to the United States. Education also changed him so that he could not return to his land, the land of his birth, the house of his father.

In Libya he had been raised to distrust Jews, even to despise them, though he never encountered them. Nearly all of Libya's Jews had left after Israel achieved statehood in 1948, but after Israel's decisive victory in the Six-Day War, anti-Jewish and anti-Zionist sentiment (one and the same in Libya) intensified. Raised in that atmosphere, Ed came to the United States, experiencing cognitive dissonance between the Jews he was taught to hate and those he encountered in his university's classrooms and laboratories.

He was open enough to let his journey take him where it was to take him—to encounter the enemy as a person. That courageous openness transformed his life in ways he could not have imagined, in large part because he encountered a Jewish woman who was equally open to him, and a rabbi and community that welcomed him with open arms.

William James, in his *Varieties of Religious Experience*, distinguishes between the "once born" and the "twice born." My Judaism is that of a "once born," a natural inheritance from my parents and theirs before them, a tradition transmitted to me by teachers and community, from my land, the place of my birth, the house of my father. Jewish tradition was the first language of depth that I encountered; the melodies of my childhood were deepened by the adult sensibilities I have developed. At times, particularly in those moments when the theology of the prayers I recite challenges the world I inhabit, I return to the native belief of my childhood, suspending disbelief, at least for a time.

Ed is a "twice born"—at least a twice, perhaps many more times than that. He stands at a distance from his childhood, the world of his youth, the community and tradition that shaped him. He came to our tradition as an adult, already with a family and a sense of self. He experiences that community and that tradition as the goal of a long journey; he encountered it as transformation and not just continuity.

The Talmud wisely states that "In the place of one who returns"—*teshuvah* means repentance, but more basically return—"even the righteous cannot stand." I am certainly not righteous but I am deeply indebted to Ed, whose story has enriched my experience and deepened my community. I cherish him as a man and revere the place where he stands.

Michael Berenbaum
Los Angeles, California

Prologue

It's a beautiful, sunny morning in Los Angeles, and I'm thinking about my grandmother. I drive with my wife and our son and daughter from our home in the Pico-Robertson neighborhood. We head west to the 405 Freeway, then make our way north, passing Westwood as we climb the Santa Monica Mountains toward Bel Air. I am filled with anticipation and gratitude.

I have been eagerly looking forward to this day—February 25, 2008—for eighteen months, but the truth is that my whole life has been pointing to this morning. You might say it was predestined. That's what my grandmother would have said—my Jida Gazalla, who encouraged my imagination and who, with her calm demeanor and wisdom, taught me how to be human. "Your life has been written in the back of your head since your birth," she used to tell me. "Just trust yourself and all will end up well."

But my life has led to places she could never have imagined when I was a child in a tiny village in the remote desert of Libya. Like Bel Air, where I pull into a parking lot at the American Jewish University and the four of us make our way into a classroom. There, the sunlight pours in through floor-to-ceiling windows as I sit, surrounded by my family and some close friends. Three elderly men walk in, two using walkers. They constitute a *beit din*, a Jewish court of rabbis. Despite their advanced years, this morning they each seem as jubilant as I feel.

For a short time, the three men pepper me with questions

about myself and my background. And then the presiding rabbi asks me the main question I have come to answer: Why, at the age of 56, have I taken on this challenging and unexpected journey? Why, in other words, do I want to be a Jew?

For a few minutes, I cannot respond. I sit in utter silence. It's not that I don't have an answer, just that I am joyfully overwhelmed by the moment. Warm tears run down my cheeks and what I feel in my heart is that somehow my fragmented past, my inquisitive present, and my hopeful future have momentarily interconnected to shed insight and give me meaning and comfort. In short, this is what I have been searching for all of my life.

This book is my answer to that question. It's the story I could not fully articulate in that moment but knew in my heart. It is my attempt to explain what I have learned about the potential for goodness inside every human heart, mind, and soul. It's my small way of encouraging people to trust their best inclinations and, in their own ways, to repair our fractured world.

In telling my story, I do not intend to disparage, belittle, or condemn any religion, faith, culture, or tradition. If I have unintentionally done so in any way, let me offer my apologies in advance.

Reflecting on my life has made me more aware of the blessing of the present moment. May we live in the present, with full awareness of our emotions moment by moment, in this place where time and space is one and the same. Then, our human difficulties become surmountable, our anxieties diminish, and our abundant love flourishes.

May your life journey be for a blessing and may your good deeds be an inspiration for courage and achievements to reduce suffering in our world.

CHAPTER 1

A Dot in the Sahara

———∞∞∞———

In the village where I grew up, we were all familiar with one taboo: it was forbidden to marry outside of your race.

Hatiet Bergen was a dot in the Sahara Desert of Libya, five-hundred miles south of Tripoli. It was a tiny community, a few dozen mud huts on the outskirts of a slightly less tiny village known as Bergen. The entire population was fewer than four hundred people. But human beings always find ways to divide themselves. In Hatiet Bergen, people drew distinctions between those of us with dark skin and those with darker skin. We were further divided into seven tribes: the Meshalish, the Gurna, the Hootmans, the Za'wide, the Al'Shabayniah, the Al'Manaseer, and the Al'Azaimeyah.

Then there were the lines of gender: men and women occupied largely separate realms. Women covered their bodies in colorful robes, wrapped their heads in brightly colored scarves, and adorned themselves in silver and beaded jewelry. Many had facial tattoos. The men wore loose cotton shirts and trousers and covered themselves in loose-fitting cloaks and flat-topped caps. Girls were schooled only for a few years, after which they worked around the house and village and waited for marriage.

Conditions were harsh—searing heat most of the year, bitter cold in the winter—and most people aspired to not much more than surviving.

We were all equally poor, with each family trying to raise crops on its own plot of sandy soil and tending to its own meager flock of sheep and goats. Still, those with lighter shades of skin enjoyed an elevated social status over people with darker skin. Sensitive to that social reality, my father frequently cautioned me against too much sun exposure. "You'll turn dark," he would say, "and look like a slave."

Besides the delineations of family, tribe, and complexion, one's fate was also determined by the role one's family played in the community. My father's family, the Elhaderis, were merchants. For as far back as anyone could remember, they had been the ones to venture from the village and bring back the staples upon which we all depended: olive oil, flour, spices, and the like. My mother's family, the Salems, were responsible for a different realm. They managed birth and death records, kept track of property lines and deeds, and served as mediators when conflicts arose between families or individuals in the village.

My father's family may have had roots in Turkey. I heard inklings that some number of our ancestors had somehow made their way from there to Fezzan, our region of south-central Libya. But the world I knew as a child was limited and isolated: outsiders rarely arrived, and locals rarely left.

Like every other couple in our village, my parents came together through an arranged marriage. (In fact, they were first cousins: my mother's father and my father's mother were siblings.)

Often parents would match up their offspring when they

were three or four years old.

With such a small population to choose from and so many restrictions of clan and tribe, the arrangement was often no more complex than identifying a child of the opposite gender of approximately the same age. Still, despite the unlikelihood that such a pairing would bring together a pair of soulmates, divorce was rare. After all, in such a small, insulated world, what options would people have once they split up? Where would they find new partners?

The early years of my parents' life together were full of pain. By the time I was a young boy, my mother and father had endured the deaths of three children, two boys and a girl, each younger than seven years of age. Those sorts of devastating losses were hardly rare in the village. Water was scarce, muddy, and unsanitary; healthcare was practically nonexistent; nutrition was lacking; the summer heat was punishing; and in winter, the crude structures offered little protection from the elements.

In the wake of these tragic losses, my father's relatives offered little consolation. In fact, some of them reacted by making my mother feel that the death was somehow her fault and predicting aloud that if she were to conceive again, she would probably have yet another child die. It was just her luck, her lot in life.

When my mother did get pregnant again—with me—she was so traumatized by her previous losses that she prayed obsessively for my health, silently bargaining with Allah to spare the child she was carrying in her womb this time. One night during the pregnancy, she experienced a vivid and intense dream: an angel paid her a visit, offering assurance that the baby would be healthy and strong and that she should call him Abdulhafied, Arabic for "servant of the protector."

As the family legend goes, I arrived on a winter morning, at dawn, during a camel caravan. Grateful and superstitious, my mother followed the angel's directions and named me Abdulhafied Elhaderi. Anxious about protecting her newborn from the harsh desert elements, she smothered my skin with olive oil, a precious commodity.

The date of my birth was never recorded. My birth certificate lists only the year, 1951, and the name of our village. It wasn't part of the culture to celebrate birthdays or keep track of ages. (Instead of years, people referred to milestones—an incident in a feud between families, perhaps, or a particularly memorable sandstorm.) My best guess is that I was born in December of 1951, which also happened to be the month that Libya gained its independence.

MY FIRST MEMORY IS OF MY CIRCUMCISION, WHEN I WAS AROUND two years old. I don't recall the pain, but I remember the celebration, the festive atmosphere. Sunni Islam doesn't prescribe a particular time for circumcision. In our village it usually happened when a child was at least a year old— sometimes as old as ten or twelve.

A circumcision called for an elaborate celebration, an opportunity for a family to welcome the entire village into its home. Families went to great efforts, slaughtering sheep or goats in order to offer a feast that fed whatever throngs showed up for the occasion. Since that also meant taking on considerable expense, families would often combine a circumcision with another significant event. In my case, the circumcision ceremony coincided with the wedding of my uncle Abdullah, my father's younger brother.

That joyous, albeit early, celebration may stand out in my memory because my primary impressions of Hatiet Bergen are of being surrounded by death. Disease seemed to strike constantly, suddenly, and randomly, leaving entire households stricken. Over and over I saw the families around me lose children to illness, and watched the entire village gather together, not so much to offer comfort as to ask desperate and painful questions: *Why is this happening to us? Why are we being punished? How can we go on?* For hours on end, women robbed of their offspring would wail in pain and disbelief. No one offered counsel or tried to provide the salve of a theological explanation. There were just tears and pain, freely and openly expressed.

As a young boy, I was far more aware of death than of birth. While families and the entire village would mark deaths with lengthy periods of communal grief, they hardly celebrated births. Perhaps that was because doing so seemed premature, or a lure to the forces of darkness. After all, it was common for infants and children to die young. Why tempt the fates?

I was around two years old when my older brother, Belgassim, died at age five. My parents placed his corpse in the middle of our living room, covering it with a white cloth. Even after they removed the body, the spot on the mud floor where they had washed it remained for several days. Every time I noticed it, I felt pangs of fear and dread.

Not long after that, my grandmother—my father's mother—died. In response, women dressed in black garments sat in front of our house, wailing in pain. The Muslim tradition was to bury the body by sunset, so almost immediately after she breathed her last breath, a group of women gathered to sew up the white burial clothing for my grandmother. They placed her lifeless body on a simple wooden carrier, and then several men hoisted it on their shoulders and carried it to the cemetery for burial. I watched from afar as another group of men dug a grave, then gathered around to lower my grandmother's body into the ground.

Death wasn't hidden. One day, I would hear word that a neighbor was sick. The next, the person would die. The family carried the corpse out of the house to the cemetery that bordered the village. Then for months after, passing that house, or playing hide-and-seek nearby, I felt twinges of trauma as I relived the ghastly images.

Present as it was in our daily lives, people rarely talked about death. Nobody made an effort to help children process their feelings or cope with their fears. Perhaps living in that tight-knit community offered the vague reassurance that I wasn't facing these things on my own, but routinely seeing and hearing women moaning and wailing certainly took its toll.

As it happened, the village cemetery bordered on the small plot of land where my family did its farming. Every time I worked that land, I would look up toward the grave-yard and feel shaken by angst and fear. Still, I spent long hours examining the cemetery. The tradition was to mark the graves of males with large stones at the two ends of the plot; a female's grave had an additional stone at the center. Families would visit a grave once annually, marking the occasion with chants accompanied by drumming on a wide drum called a *bendir* and the lighting of *louban* incense.

I sometimes heard stories of unfortunate people who were buried alive. According to the frightening rumors that circulated among us children, there was a way to confirm this: weeks after a burial, cracks would appear on surface atop the burial plot—presumably caused by their screams for help.

Night could be a scary time to be near the cemetery. The villagers had powerful superstitions about ghosts, so I didn't dare venture out alone on moonless nights. I heard stories about a courageous man who wanted to dispel superstitions by going at midnight to the cemetery, where he would hammer a post into the ground, leaving it for everyone to observe by daylight the next day. He was in such a hurry that he accidentally hammered part of his clothing to it and couldn't extricate himself. The poor man thought ghosts had gotten ahold of him and the experience drove him insane. For the rest of his days, he was known as the village's *majnoon*, its insane person.

THEN THERE WERE THE VERY REAL HAZARDS OF LIFE IN THE village: the wild creatures that lived among us. It was the custom to post writings from the Quran, wrapped in palm leaves, in the doorways of households, as a sort of amulet to ward off scorpions and snakes.

That practice had only mixed results. People routinely stepped on scorpions in the dark of night, suffering stings that were potentially lethal. When that happened, they would call one particular villager, a man who would use a sharp knife to cut into the skin and then suck out the venom with his mouth. I always marveled at how strong and healthy he must have been to tolerate that poison over and over again.

In the village, medical care was primitive at best—and at worst, misguided and dangerous. When I was four years old I developed a stomachache that showed no improvement, even after several days. One morning I woke up in my grandmother's house to find my family gathered around me. My mother was heating up something on the stove, next to the pot of tea. Before I realized what was happening, someone held my body down while my mother took a white-hot iron rod and pressed it into my body just above my navel, burning a cross into my skin. The pain was excruciating. I couldn't imagine why my loved ones would harm me in this way.

Later, I learned that this was a common folk-medicine practice in the region, known as *kawi*. People believed that branding the skin with these hot implements had curative effects. Of course, the opposite was true. My mother used *kawi* many times—on my back, neck, and head—with the mistaken notion that she was curing ailments. Each time, it took several months for the burned spot to heal, and each time I was left with a lasting scar. (Many years later I would find it impossible to explain these bodily artifacts to physicians half a world away.)

Along with these physically painful episodes, I endured other experiences that left me psychologically scarred—and confused. From an early age, for example, I was witness to an occasional exorcism. When I was around five years old, my mother would sometimes enter an altered state of consciousness, speaking in a high-pitched voice, apparently the voice of some spirit that had possessed her. As I watched, it was difficult to comprehend what was going on. Usually she would call upon her brother, my Uncle Mashri, who would come and confront the spirit, urging it to depart from my mother's body. He would plead for hours, as incense, known as *louban*, burned, before the spirit finally acceded, agreeing to leave and return another time. These confrontations always left my mother exhausted, relieved, and in need of many days' rest.

In fact, in the village, it wasn't unusual to see people enter altered states of consciousness. On Friday nights, a small group of men known as the Isawiyya, a brotherhood dating back to the fifteenth century, would gather in a modest structure called a *zawia* to chant rhythmically (a practice known as *dhikr*), drumming on the *bandir* while burning incense. As the chanting reached a fevered pitch, two of the men would start channeling various personalities, apparently entering altered states, running around crazily and jumping up and down. Like the other kids watching, I felt both fascinated and terrified. This would go on for an hour or more, until some of the other men would hold the hand of the one who had entered an altered state, leading them in a chant about being one with Allah and His Prophet and asking the man to submit to Allah's will. It always ended with the formerly possessed man lying flat on the ground, another person massaging his limbs and head.

With such backward medicine and with death and dangers all around, it felt like a miracle just to be alive. And perhaps it was miraculous that I survived my family, with all of its complexities.

My mother's name was Mabruka Salem. Her first name was a variation of the Arabic word for blessing, her last name the word for peace. But she was anything but a peaceful soul. Experiencing the death of one child after another had taken its toll, leaving her nervous, overly protective, and generally unhappy.

Mother had a brother and four sisters and came from a large extended family.

My father's name was Elsaidi Elhaderi. Saidi is the word for a happy person, and our family name, Elhaderi, could mean either a learned person or a person from an urban area. My father had only a single brother, my uncle Abdullah, whose wife, my aunt, was Masuda Ertima Hootmani.

I was never close to my father. He was frequently away from home for work, and I have a few scattered memories of his presence. When I was very young he would read from the one religious book he owned, a volume containing all of the Muslim names of God. I would watch him intently as he chanted the names, one after another, seemingly in an altered state of consciousness.

I watched with fascination as he went about his mundane household tasks. My father would shave his face—wrinkled from exposure to the desert climate—with a dull metal blade that he sharpened by rubbing it on the inside of a glass. The process always left some cuts, and he would wipe the blood from his face with an old rag.

He didn't speak much, and when he did, his statements were often cryptic. When we were at home or walking together in the village and I asked him to explain why he had done something, or why he owned a particular object, he had a strange, standard answer: "It is for the dogs when they come barking." I never understood what he meant, and the odd response always annoyed and frustrated me.

In moments of anger, too, he would act out without bothering to explain himself. When I was six, I was once visiting my grandmother's house and stayed longer than my parents expected, not realizing that my parents were at home, waiting for me to return for lunch. When I finally left,

I was halfway home when I encountered my father, who was out looking for me. Without uttering a word, he slapped my face, leaving me stunned and confused. The two of us walked back home in silence.

Despite his distant and taciturn nature, we occasionally shared joyful moments. One evening when I was seven, my father was preparing to join some relatives on an overnight camel caravan to an oasis, where they planned to gather wood and harvest the fruit of date palm trees. When I asked if I could go along, he said no. But when they departed for the journey, I secretly followed the group from behind. As they reached the outskirts of the village and were preparing to mount the camels, I called out to my father. I was terrified that he would react in anger, or at least send me home. Instead, he agreed to let me come along on the journey. I hadn't brought any extra clothing, and—even more problematic—I was barefoot and had no shoes. With daytime temperatures soaring above 120 degrees Fahrenheit, it would have been brutal on my feet, so my father crafted shoes for me from palm fronds.

In spite of those harsh conditions, I enjoyed the adventure, particularly the evening when the entire group gathered at an oasis to prepare dinner in the moonlight. It proved to be one of my few happy memories of time with my father.

Early in my life, he worked in his family's business, a small store that my grandparents ran out of their home where they sold staples such as olive oil, kerosene, rice, and pasta. Customers would pay by credit or sometimes by barter. He would travel as far as Tripoli to purchase goods. Once or twice a year a truck would arrive to deliver merchandise.

For reasons I never understood, my father left the family business when I was around six years old and landed a series of government jobs, most of them as a supervisor for road workers. For much of my childhood, he would travel to remote places where roads were under construction. There, he sat in the shade and supervised a crew of a dozen or so as they paved or patched roads.

I was around ten when my father was working as an after-hours security guard at a government grain facility in Sebha, the nearest large city. He brought me to join him for the summer. What could have been an awful couple of months became much more entertaining because of a nearby government junkyard, where I explored freely and discovered, to my delight, a large number of discarded automobiles. I spent countless hours that summer playing amidst the debris, climbing into the immobile cars and pretending to drive. My Uncle Abdullah was working nearby at a large government ranch and dairy where he cared for cows used to produce milk for the area's more affluent residents. There, too, I had the freedom to roam—among the cows and other livestock.

Those experiences notwithstanding, my father and I had a mostly distant relationship. Perhaps the deaths of three children before me made him hesitant to forge a close bond with me, lest he lose me, too. If so, I never heard him talk about that. In fact, he rarely spoke at all. When he was displeased with me, sometimes I knew only because he would give me a whack.

He was demanding, constantly expecting me to perform chores that were normally done by adults—work with our family's crops, for instance, or tending to sheep or camels. When I was still quite young, he would send me to collect debts from people who owed him money or to ask for favors or loans that he was uncomfortable requesting on his own.

Sometimes he sent me to ask neighbors for tobacco or tea leaves. The tasks felt awkward and difficult, but I had no choice; he was the father and I was the son.

I always sensed tension between my parents. Undoubtedly, the death of their children had scarred them both, with the blame and recriminations that often come with enduring such pain. Sometimes my father would return from long stretches away from the village for work, and my mother would seek refuge with her mother to avoid him. Still, divorce was unheard of—and surely their separation would have been traumatic for me.

I WAS SIX YEARS OLD WHEN MY MOTHER BECAME PREGNANT AND seven when she delivered. I was alone at home with her around dusk when she went into labor. I didn't fully understand what was happening to my mother, but we were sitting together in the living room when she became visibly uncomfortable. Suddenly, I noticed water flowing from her body and soaking the sand-covered floor. As she screamed in pain, I noticed something fall to the floor, similar to what I had observed at the births of animals.

"Abdulhafied!" she shouted. "Run and get someone to help me!"

I followed her instructions and summoned neighbors. Very quickly, the house filled up with friends and relatives. Amidst the noise and excitement of the adults, I fell asleep.

My parents named my brother Abdullatif, meaning "servant of the gentle." (In Islam, Latif is one of the names of God.) With the disparity in our ages, we weren't close. Abdullatif had his own friends and I had mine. Once, when he was about three and I was ten, we were playing together in a large cardboard box. I was enjoying the role of older brother, playing a variation on "Simon Says," issuing commands that he would follow. Then my mother arrived and Abdullatif suddenly burst into tears.

"Abdulhafied was bossing me around!" he told her. "I don't like it!"

She scolded me. I felt sad that my little brother had so misinterpreted my efforts to entertain him.

Since my father was away for much of my childhood, my Uncle Mashri, my mother's brother, often stood in for him as parent and protector for our family. Mashri was much gentler than my father, with a warmth that was a contrast to my father's harsh and distant manner. If Uncle Mashri disapproved of something I did, he would indicate it with a certain look that sent the message clearly but didn't do damage in the process.

While my immediate family brought its share of discomfort and difficulty, I did have one adult relative who was a constant source of comfort, joy, and love: my maternal grandmother, my Jida Gazalla. I never knew my grandfathers, and my paternal grandmother died when I was still a toddler. But I spent most of my nights as a child sleeping at my *jida's* home. She had a remarkable ability to calm down practically anyone.

The best part of staying with *Jida* was that every night she would share bedtime stories: long, mesmerizing tales that stretched over weeks and months. I always struggled to stay awake and alert as I listened to her narrate these fairytales in her sweet, soothing voice. Her telling was so imaginative and engaging that I lay in the dark, picturing every prince and princess, every castle, every moment. But I could fight off sleep for only so long, usually nodding off in mid-story. Jida Gazalla would pick up where she left off the following night. At that rate, she would take half a year to tell a single, protracted story. When she got to the end, Jida Gazalla would start again from the beginning and tell it all over again.

My grandmother also played an important role in the village, as a sort of self-made therapist to any neighbors who found their way to her door. No matter what the problem— marital dispute, illness, conflict between neighbors—she could soothe the visitor's nerves, offer some perspective, and assure the person that everything would work out. She had an openness about her, an acceptance of all kinds of people, that was rare and that left a lasting impression on me.

My grandmother didn't counsel in an official capacity. It was simply her talent, her gift. When I stayed with her, I watched people come and go all day. She would wave the visitor in, sit down with the person, listen intently, and offer words of support. Everyone seemed to depart calmer, less agitated, and a little bit wiser.

THAT KIND OF SPONTANEOUS VISITING WASN'T UNUSUAL IN THE village. In fact, it was the norm. The houses had doors, but they were designed not to keep people out, but to block animals from entering the residences. Humans, on the other hand, flowed freely into and out of each other's homes naturally and casually. We had no concept of retreating to private quarters and shutting out others. Houses were considered nearly as much public domains as any other space.

That was certainly true of our house. Like every other home in Hatiet Bergen, it was a crude, circular structure, with mud-brick walls and a thatched roof made of a lattice of palm fronds.

The entire house covered about three hundred square feet. The front door led into a large courtyard, from which another door opened to the main living space, a compact room we all shared. The heat source was a fire pit, a small hole in the ground at the center of the main room. We had no beds; the entire family slept on rugs around the fire. Our pillows consisted of clothing stuffed into cloth sacks. The tiny kitchen area in one corner was where we stored a few pots and pans for cooking, our dishes, and the firewood. In another corner was a small, separate area for storage.

The houses in Hatiet Bergen felt ancient, but the oldest structures dated back perhaps five decades. As a child, I sometimes explored with other little boys beyond the village boundaries, and we sometimes came upon a cluster of older, deteriorated mud houses, partially buried in sand, victims of decades—or centuries—of desert sandstorms. Nothing manmade lasted forever in the harsh Sahara climate.

Every house was a communal project. When a family needed a new home, the entire village would contribute to the effort, following the same steps each time: using molds to form bricks from mud; carrying them by hand or donkey to the site; stacking the bricks to create exterior walls of seven feet or so; and cutting old palm trees into studs that served as rafters, supporting the palm-frond ceiling.

The roof was sufficient to protect us from the harsh desert sun, but when rains came—just once or twice a year, but hard and driving rains—the water easily penetrated the thatched roof, soaking us and everything inside.

Like every other house in our village, ours had neither a toilet nor a bathroom. (The practice was just to find a place outdoors, squat and do one's business. The common clothing, a long white shirt called a *soriya*, lent some sense of privacy; men wore an extra outer layer called *jarid*.) And with water scarce and no indoor plumbing, most men would bathe with water only rarely, perhaps twice a year. It was more common for women to bring a pitcher of water into the house for whatever personal washing they needed.

The entire village fit within about a square mile, surrounded by plots designated for each extended family for farming seasonal crops: barley, wheat, corn, onions, garlic, and tomatoes.

Each family also maintained a small herd of animals: sheep, goats, and camels, with donkeys designated to do the heavy lifting and hauling. When sandstorms would occasionally leave the fields buried under a foot or two of sand, the family would use a donkey to help sweep the sand away, rescuing the crops underneath.

Animals also did the work of drawing the water from the handful of wells surrounding the village using a *dalow*, a special bucket made from sheep skin. It was the women's job to carry water from the well to the home, balancing the large jugs atop their heads, which were usually wrapped in colorful cloths. The young, unmarried women would sometimes intentionally moisten their cloths in order to show off the contours of their bodies and to illicit gossip about being ready for marriage.

I grew up quickly. With such a small population in our village, everyone's help was significant and needed. Children were expected to take an active role in helping the family and the tribe. Sitting at home doing nothing simply wasn't an option. At two, I was responsible for feeding the chickens and other livestock early each morning. By age four, my job was to gather the larger animals in the fields and escort them back to the house. At seven, I had learned to shear sheep, using a special pair of scissors so large that it required two of my undersized hands to manage the task. (We used the wool to make blankets, rugs, and special fabrics for circumcisions and weddings.) By age ten, I was slaughtering sheep and goats; I had picked up that skill by watching the process over and over again. With commodities so scarce, we made use of every part of the animal: milk, bones, hide, meat. Nothing was wasted.

THE TREE OF LIFE IN THE VILLAGE WAS THE DATE PALM tree, *nakhla*. There would have been no life without it—it was as essential as water and air. It was forbidden to cut down a palm tree unless it hadn't produced dates for two years, or if the dates' quality was notably poor. We utilized every part of the tree in everyday products. The trees provided shade from the scorching sun. The dates sustain humans and animals alike: the pits could be crushed to fatten male sheep for slaughter on special occasions such as circumcisions, weddings, and Eid Alkabir, the holiday marking the end of the *hajj* season. We used palm fronds to cover roofs, as cooking wood, to build barriers to protect farm plots from sandstorms, to make storage containers and serving plates, to make sleeping mats, and also to fashion drinking cups. We used the leafy mesh to make fine and thick ropes for a variety of purposes. *Harjoon*, the fresh yellow branches that carried dates, were used for building material, cooking wood and to make noisemakers kids used to celebrate Ramadan, the fasting month, and Mawlud, the commemoration of the Prophet's birthdate. The tree trunks were used in home construction as rafters, doors, and door frames and for building the frame to collect water from wells for drinking and irrigation. We made fans and shoes from the fronds.

The palms' dates were also used as tea sweetener and to make *uhmada*, the fermented fluid to fashion flour into dough and baking bread. The date palm was even a source of toys and games. As a child I spent a great deal of time playing a game we called *tat*, using date pits as game pieces. The largest piece, polished and smooth on top, was the king, known as Tat. Each player started with an equal number of date pits. We threw them on the floor, and the goal was to remove all of the pits, known as soldiers, without touching the king.

Central to life, palms trees were also part of death: we used their trunks as frames to carry the dead to the *gubr*, the final resting place.

NOT EVERYONE PRAYED AS REQUIRED FIVE TIMES A DAY. BUT ALL of us, young and old, drank tea three times a day—and a fourth time on special days, when the family gathered to welcome a visitor. It was a meditative ceremony that helped people to relax and share family and village gossip.

The ceremony had three specific steps. Some individuals were known around the village for their mastery of the tea ceremony, and families would call on them to make the occasion extra memorable. Tea was an essential cultural commodity in Libya, central to family gatherings. A meal wasn't considered complete without a three-round tea ceremony. A wedding without a continuous flow of tea for seven days would be considered a failure, as disastrous as a non-virgin bride. Even when people traveled for weeks on a camel caravan, packing tea and its implements was as important as bringing water. Even our house cat, which was rarely sociable, often hiding all day, would calmly sit by the warm kerosene lantern as part of the evening family gathering. One tradition that emerged across Libya and became a national pastime was adding roasted peanuts to a warm cup of tea to enhance the flavor to a level of ecstasy.

Once when I was around five, I woke up early one morning at my grandmother's house when the family was lighting the fire for warmth and for tea. My uncle Mashri had acquired some raw peanuts from a friend. I sat next to him, trying to shell the peanuts. He watched me struggle with them, then smiled at me, his eyes sparkling. "There is always a natural and easy way to do everything," he said.

Kindly and deliberately, Uncle Mashri showed me how to shell a peanut, and I was excited to see how easy it was. As he roasted the peanuts on the open fire next to the teapot, the aroma sweetened the air like an expensive perfume.

I would go through significant transformations and many cultural changes later in life, but dates would remain my favorite candy and tea with roasted peanuts my soothing drink.

IN THE TABLEAU OF AGRICULTURAL PLOTS AND ROUGH-HEWN shelters that made up our village, one structure stood out: a white building constructed of reinforced concrete and a real roof—not palm fronds, but concrete. Amidst the mud houses and unpaved roadways, it stood out like a palace, but it didn't belong to royalty or the rich. It was the school.

Libya became an independent nation in 1951, the same year I was born. It was a poor nation, struggling to feed its citizens. Its constitution, drafted with input from the United Nations, placed a strong emphasis on education as the way to uplift Libya's citizens and, in turn, its economy. The local school in Hatiet Bergen was among hundreds the government built as part of that effort.

My formal education began before I ever set foot in the school. When I turned four, I began learning at the Quranic school. For two or three hours each day, an imam instructed us in the basics of reading and writing. Each child had a *loah*, a small wooden slate, and we used *samag*, home-made ink derived from fatty clumps of sheep wool (similar to the ink used by Torah scribes). Once we learned the alphabet, he instructed us to copy the words of verses from the Quran: first short verses, then longer ones, until we mastered the process. Performing these drills over and over, we learned through imitation and repetition the fundamentals of reading and writing.

I had a number of cousins who were two or three years older than I and already attending the new school. Watching them come and go to school and work at their assignments made me jealous and eager to join in on what was going on in the impressive white building.

When I reached age five and finally started at the school, one of the immediate bonuses was food. Every day the school served lunch, the kinds of food we didn't get at home: tuna, biscuits, a slice of a moldy cheddar cheese, powdered milk—mostly supplied by American humanitarian organizations such as CARE USA. One of the teachers would heat a huge bucket of water every afternoon to mix with powder to make milk he would distribute to us in cups.

The principal was a relative on my mother's side. Most of that generation in our village hadn't received much formal education, but somehow this man had reached a level adequate to oversee a school.

Though it was by far the largest structure in the village, the school had just four rooms: three classrooms and another used for storage and as a teachers' workspace. Given those limitations and six grades, one teacher was responsible for two or three grades at once: the third graders would sit in one row of seats, the fourth graders in the next. That required teachers to be flexible and versatile, switching among students at different levels and with different curricula throughout the day.

HATIET BERGEN WAS SO ISOLATED THAT WE RARELY SAW A MOTOR VEHICLE. When one did arrive, it was a big event, especially among the children, who would gather around to examine and admire the car or truck. Most often it was a Land Rover, the most common form of motorized transportation in the desert. Cars were so expensive and so rare in our part of the desert that often those that did come or go from the village were packed with people. First, they would load up a car with suitcases or duffel bags or boxes, and then a dozen people might ride as passengers, some crammed inside, some hanging on the exterior, their hands gripping a strap or bar so as not to fall off.

As a child, I had little awareness of the world beyond my village, and even less understanding of whatever went on beyond my immediate surroundings. We received no newspapers or magazines. Now and then one of the locals would journey to Tripoli and come back with stories that sounded fantastical. Occasionally an airplane would fly high overhead, so high above that it would appear as a tiny dot moving through the night sky. Watching, I would wonder: Who was on that plane? Where were they coming from? Where were they headed? And would I ever see the lands and adventures and people that lay beyond my village?

The only books I saw were school textbooks, which focused on mathematics and basic science but didn't delve into current events. In fourth grade, we began learning geography, which gave me my first glimpses of the world beyond our corner of the Sahara Desert, beyond Libya.

I was around five years old the first time I heard a radio. One of my cousins had a large block radio with an external battery as big as the radio itself. It could receive a signal only at night, and it seemed the entire village would gather outside the family's house, listening to newscasts or music broadcast by Cairo Radio or the two Libyan stations—one from Tripoli, the other from Benghazi. (It would be many years before I would experience television.)

Our family was poor by any standard, but as a child I didn't think in those terms. Nearly everyone we knew lived in similar conditions, with similar resources. People worked hard, not to accumulate wealth, but merely to survive and get through each day.

I had little understanding of the meaning of money. When I was five, I needed an ink pen so that I could do my schoolwork, so I begged my mother to buy me one. She finally agreed, handing me a single paper dinar and instructing me to go to the small village store.

"But don't forget to bring me the change!" she called after me as I dashed out the door.

Excited, I ran all the way to the store, handed the merchant the cash, and asked him for a blue-ink pen. He gave me a pen and a handful of coins, warning me to wrap the coins and pen in the corner of my long *soriya* so that I wouldn't lose them. "I don't want your mother to think I didn't give you correct change," he said.

Overjoyed to have the pen, I hurried back home, where my mother carefully examined the coins I handed her. "Where's the rest of the change?" she asked. "Half the coins that should be here are missing!"

I shrugged. She shook her head. "Abdulhafied, I want you to go straight back to the merchant and tell him to give you the correct change."

Less eager this time—I was barefoot and it was a hot summer day—I walked back from our house to the store.

"What can I do for you now?" he said.

I told him that my mother wanted the rest of the change for her dinar.

He shook his head. "I gave you the correct change. I told you not to lose it."

Back at home, I tried to explain that to my mother. She wasn't happy.

"Go find the coins," she said. "I want you to retrace your steps, look everywhere you walked between here and the store and find the coins."

She made it sound easy, as if I could magically find the change on the ground. But I walked—this time more deliberately—from home back to the merchant, but could not find the money. It was a difficult way to learn the importance of being careful with money—every cent.

TWO OR THREE TIMES A YEAR, A TRUCK ARRIVED FROM CARE USA, a humanitarian organization that delivered packages containing food, clothing, and household items. As soon as it approached, someone alerted the town: "CARE! CARE! The truck is coming!" It was an event, a scene. We children ran out of our homes to greet the truck, running after it to try to latch ourselves on for a ride.

The bed of the truck was loaded with provisions. Half of it was food: staples such as sacks of flour or barley or rice, powdered milk, or blocks of cheese. The other half was shoes, clothing, and household items such as blankets.

The driver always pulled to a stop in a central place, where one local resident was designated to represent the village and help distribute the goods. Representatives of the various families lined up, and the local representative listed their needs: "The Elhaderi family needs four pairs of shoes, seven blankets, ten sacks of flour…" No one argued or pleaded. The families accepted what they received. After the truck pulled away, families sometimes bartered with each other, so the family that most needed a particular item would get it. Much of the food was designated for the kitchen of the school, where each day they would serve us lunch, typically consisting of things such as canned tuna, crackers, and cheese.

Like most kids, I watched adults closely and often tried to imitate their behavior. So many adults around me smoked cigarettes that my friends and I would sometimes play pretend, rolling up dried tea leaves in discarded pieces of paper. When I was six a neighbor who smoked tobacco in a pipe asked me if I really wanted to try it. I said yes, so he packed his pipe heavily with tobacco and told me to take a strong hit. After a few minutes, he left me alone, feeling the ground spinning around me. He probably thought he was offering me some kind of life lesson. But his foolishness could have caused serious harm, or even cost me my life.

One summer when I was around five years old, a man arrived in the village with a flock of sheep that he hoped to sell to the local residents. To help him tend the sheep, he had a white dog with him. We rarely got visitors, and I had never seen a dog, nor had most of my friends. We were all fascinated with it, and we reacted like typical boys. While the man was sitting in the shade with some of the local adults negotiating sheep prices, we made attempts to play with the dog. None of us knew what to do, so we called after it. When that proved ineffective, we started tossing stones and sticks in its direction—anything to get its attention.

Finally, in the late afternoon, the man concluded his business. He had sold very few sheep—if any—so he started making his way out beyond the village boundaries, his dog accompanying him to herd the sheep. A group of us, still fascinated with the dog, tagged along. Undeterred, we kept following the man and his flock for a mile or so beyond the village. Some of the boys heedlessly pestering the dog, shouting after it, and throwing things in its direction. Finally, the man grew annoyed, and he shouted something to the dog. At that moment, the dog turned around and suddenly dashed in our direction.

Terrified, we turned to flee. The other boys got ahead of me. I simply couldn't run fast enough to outpace the dog, so I was straggling behind them, the last in our group. Suddenly, I felt a sharp pain in my thigh, then tumbled to the ground, grasping my leg in agonizing pain. The dog had bitten me, then turned back and rejoined its master and the flock of sheep.

In shock, I managed to limp back to the village and to my home. I wasn't bleeding—to this day, I don't understand how that could have been—but there was a deep hole in my thigh. My mother and father tried tending to me, but over a number of days, the pain only increased, and I developed an infection and, later, a ferocious fever. My thigh grew so swollen and sore that I could not walk, and the fever became so elevated that I was sweating in agony.

My life was in danger. With no medical care available, the only option was to seek outside help. My Uncle Mashri, my mother's brother, volunteered to seek assistance at the clinic in Bergen, about seven miles from our home. He traveled there using the fastest means possible: donkey. It would likely take an entire day for him to make the journey, get help, and return to the village.

I was lying in bed, still in agony, when he returned, accompanied by another man, a nurse from Bergen's medical clinic. The nurse pulled something out of his bag: a syringe with a needle that looked as long and thick as a nail. That terrified me, but the nurse assured me it was necessary, and that it would help me. I closed my eyes tightly and tensed my entire body as he gave me the injection in my buttocks.

Within a day or so, the fever subsided. The medication had successfully curbed the infection—and probably saved my life. My recovery, though, was slow and drawn out. My body was weak and fragile, and I had to spend a couple of months at home in bed as my worried mother cared for me. Over time, I regained my health and strength. In time I could walk again and, though the scar remained, the wound slowly healed.

Uncle Mashri, always my best advocate and protector, was infuriated by the recklessness the sheep dealer had shown in siccing his dog on my friends and me. He insisted on taking action, so sometime after I was back on my feet, the two of us traveled by donkey the seven miles to the village of Bergen to visit the district police headquarters. There, my uncle helped me to file a police report.

The complaint failed to elicit any kind of legal action, but my uncle's concern made a big difference to me. It gave me the feeling that someone was taking care of me, that an adult in my life took me seriously, believed in me, and would be on my side.

IN OUR VILLAGE WE HAD FEW POSSESSIONS BEYOND THE MOST basic essentials—certainly not luxuries such as toys or sports equipment. All of our playthings were homemade and improvised. But when I was in second grade, the school's principal decided it was important for us to have a real soccer ball to play with, and he set out to raise money to purchase it. A ball like that would cost about fifteen dinars, so he asked each of us to appeal to our parents to donate a small amount:

one-tenth of a dinar. If each family contributed, we could raise about half the necessary funds. Collecting that much money wasn't easy. It took about four months of cajoling and pressure to gather half the funds, which were matched by the teachers and the principal himself. Finally, the principal sent the money with someone from the village making a trek to Tripoli. The designated person bought the ball and sent it on the next truck bringing food and supplies to the village.

After all those months of anticipation, we children were elated when the ball finally arrived—thick, made of light-brown leather. It even came with a bottle of grease to help reduce wear and tear. But then we tried to play with it. My first attempt to kick it with my bare feet, proved surprisingly painful. My friends felt the same way. This was the ball we had been waiting for? It was simply too hard for comfort. After all that, the ball became the favorite toy not for us kids, but for our teachers. We kids went back to our own toys and games.

I DIDN'T HAVE A LOT OF KIDS TO ADMIRE IN THE VILLAGE, BUT one of them was Ali Aabed, who was four years my senior. In our closed and isolated community, Ali was probably the first "outside-the-box" thinker I ever encountered. He was also large and strong, whereas I was small and sickly.

When Ali was twelve, he somehow created a bicycle—complete with wheels, frame, and handlebars—from nothing but products of trees. I marveled watching him ride it, fantasizing that perhaps someday he would build another for me.

About a year later, Ali became a local hero of a different sort. One cold winter morning, the entire village was awakened by an unusual, faraway noise: the screech of a donkey being attacked by a wolf. Entire families left their homes, drawn to the source of the sounds. When they got close, and the roar grew louder, though, everyone stopped. Everyone, that is, except Ali Aabed. He kept walking forward through the morning mist, armed only with a stick.

A few minutes later, the wolf's howl faded to silence. Then Ali appeared, riding the donkey. If we had a village hero, it was Ali, who adopted the donkey as his own.

Then, a couple of months later, a visitor arrived from a nearby: a man who wanted to claim that donkey. Ali refused to part with it, so the man entered intense negotiations with the village elders. Eventually, they emerged with a deal: the elders recognized Ali as a courageous man, and the original donkey owner compensated Ali for saving the donkey and caring for it. So Ali the hero finally relented.

⸰⸰⸰

ONE LATE AFTERNOON WHEN I WAS IN FOURTH GRADE, WITHOUT warning, a Land Rover pulled into the village. It dropped off two people, a man and a woman in their twenties. I could tell by their dress that they came from outside of our area, perhaps from Europe. Instead of the loose-fitting *soriya* that men in Hatiet Bergen usually wore, the man had on a button-town shirt and a blazer. The woman with him wore a blouse and skirt. I had never seen people dressed that way in real life, only in newspapers or magazines that would occasionally make their way to the village. They looked exotic and sophisticated. The driver, carrying other passengers, was in such a rush to get to his next destination that the Land Rover ran over one of their suitcases, cracking it open and exposing some of the clothing packed inside.

I soon learned that this man was to be a new school-teacher. Nobody had been expecting him, perhaps not even the school's principal. That didn't stop the adults in the village from greeting the couple with warmth and hospitality. Within hours, the locals had identified an abandoned house, cleaned it up, gathered enough donated furnishings to make it habitable, and helped the couple to settle in.

The man's name was Mahmood. We called him O'stad Mahmood, Teacher Mahmood. He and his wife were Palestinian Arabs. I was only vaguely aware of the conflict between the Jewish state of Israel and its Arab neighbors, but I did notice that the adults in the village welcomed the couple with unusual enthusiasm.

In fact, the very next morning, our principal dispatched a group of us to the nearby oasis to gather palm fronds. When we brought the branches back, some of the village men used them to add a room to the teacher's house: the village's first indoor bathroom.

As O'stad Mahmood settled into the village, I marveled at how he adapted to our way of life. It was clear from his appearance and demeanor that he had been raised in a different culture a world away from our unrefined lifestyle. I wondered, how was he able to fit in? How did he adjust to sleeping on the ground as we did? How did he get used to our food, our customs, our dirty water?

Before long, I grew close to the teacher, in part because I made myself available as a helper, assisting with household chores. I helped acquire chickens and eggs for the couple, and they came to rely on me for other tasks. Being close to the teacher provided me with a bit of status among my friends, a small bit of popularity I had not previously enjoyed.

It also had its drawbacks. After a while, O'stad Mahmood started calling me by a nickname inspired by my small stature: Gazim, from the Arabic for dwarf. The new moniker was a mixed blessing, reflecting his affection for me, but also giving the other boys ammunition for relentlessly teasing me for years after.

⸭

ANOTHER INCIDENT THAT RAISED MY PROFILE AND STATUS IN THE village was one involving my father. Every Friday after prayers at the mosque the local men would sit around chatting. One Friday afternoon when I was seven years old, my father became embroiled in an argument with another man over a rather trivial topic: the ownership of a camel. As I understood it, the men had agreed to purchase the animal jointly, but then a misunderstanding had arisen over the payments. The dispute between my father and this considerably larger man became so heated that they began physically tussling. My father came away with a scratch on his face, but he responded by expressing pride that he had stood up to the man.

The other man's son, who was my age, responded to the skirmish by writing a poem mocking my father. It quickly circulated through the village. I was so disturbed that I enlisted the help of one of my cousins. Madani, the son of my father's sister, was two years older than I, and he was the smartest boy I knew. In the village, he had a reputation for excelling in school, and, in particular, for his ability to write. Together, we wrote our own poem taking issue with the other boy's account, challenging it point by point, and portraying my father as the obvious hero. We enlisted the help of another cousin, Sharif, who was a year older, to circulate and to publicize the poem throughout the village.

The people who read our poem responded with great enthusiasm, praising our words and also coming around to our side. I collected a lot of praise for standing up for my father's integrity—and for my writing prowess. That experience gave me a sense of the power of the written word. I gained a reputation in the village as a person with a talent for writing things down, both for keeping a record of events and for using the written word to settle disputes.

CHAPTER 2

Leaving Home

⸺◦◦◦⸺

When I was eleven and finished sixth grade, it was time to move on to middle school, which was far from the village, in the town of Brak, about forty miles east of Hatiet Bergen. I didn't feel prepared to leave home: I had never ventured from the village except with my father or uncle. But it was time. My mother gave me one and a half dinars— enough for about ten loaves of bread—and sent me off with some classmates.

As if leaving home wasn't difficult enough, the journey itself was an ordeal. I was one of six boys from the village heading to Brak. But, with, no established transportation in our part of the desert, we had no choice but to simply wait for the next vehicle to arrive.

In late August, around the time the school year was to start, a truck arrived with a delivery of rice, olive oil, and other staples. Not knowing if another vehicle might come through anytime soon, someone decided that this would be our best option to get to Brak. The bed was already packed with sacks of dates bound for Tripoli's market, but the six of us piled aboard, each carrying a modest satchel of clothing.

We left in the early afternoon. The truck was so weighed

down with cargo—human and otherwise—that it could barely travel at ten miles per hour as it made its way through the desert, first stopping in the village of Bergen, where we picked up another ten boys. We continued that way, stopping in villages and picking up more passengers until more than about thirty of us had somehow crammed ourselves onto the truck. Late that night, we arrived in Brak, the central city of an area called Wadi Al Shati, a dried up oasis stretching over sixty miles that was now dotted with villages.

As it turned out, our timing was slightly off. We had arrived about a week before school was to start. The dormitory where the other boys and I were to be living hadn't yet opened for the school year, so we camped outside—our group from Hatiet Bergen, along with about fifty others who had arrived from other villages in the area. I used the money from my mother to buy enough to eat for a couple of days, but when that was gone, I grew so hungry that I was forced to beg classmates, and then locals, for food.

It was just the start of an awful year. I was always short for my age, and with my peers starting to hit adolescence and growing more rapidly, the difference became more pronounced, and I became more self-conscious about my small stature. I also felt poor, lacking adequate clothing and proper shoes. Living in the dormitory, too, was an adjustment, though I enjoyed the consistent meals, a step up from the more unpredictable diet of my early years.

Only a few weeks into the year, I developed an awful, persistent cough that grew into a full-blown illness so severe that I landed in the hospital. Just being there proved traumatic. It was a dingy, poorly heated institution in an isolated location. There was stagnant water nearby and the whole place had a nauseating, putrid odor. My bed was in a ward with about twenty other patients, and I rarely received a visitor.

Healthcare was so rudimentary that there was little the doctors and nurses could do for many patients, so I was in a ward surrounded by people who were near death, with little chance of recovery. Twice during the months of my stay, I overheard patients suffering late at night and finally succumbing to their illness.

As for me, I lay in bed coughing. The doctors gave me pills and administered shots, but nobody ever told me what my illness was, or what the prognosis was.

As if the disruption, illness, and dreadful conditions weren't challenging enough, halfway through the year, I learned that my parents had moved from our village. My father had been working in Sebha, the largest city in the Fezzan region. Apparently, he was tired of the constant travel between there and the village, so he had decided to relocate the family to a new home in one of Sebha's suburbs.

WHEN I WAS FEELING SOMEWHAT BETTER—THOUGH STILL FAR from fully recovered—a hospital employee explained to me that instead of returning to the village, I would make my way to my parents' new home, the location of which I knew only vaguely. One day the hospital's Land Rover was scheduled to transport a boy who was desperately ill to the larger hospital in Sebha, so a staffer instructed me to go along for the ride.

I had been told we would depart early in the day, but after the driver faced an unexpected delay, we weren't able to leave until late afternoon. The driver and a hospital staffer got into a heated argument about the wisdom of hitting the road so late in the day, but eventually, we hit the road heading from Brak out into the desert.

The late departure turned out to be a bad idea after all. Some ten miles outside of Brak, the Land Rover stalled, and the driver, growing frustrated, was helpless to get it started again. Instead of making our way to Sebha, we sat in the pitch dark, praying that another vehicle would come in that direction carrying someone who might be able to lend help.

From there, things got even worse. While we waited in the darkness, the boy we were supposed to be transporting to Sebha's hospital died. The driver, with nothing else to do, covered the boy's lifeless body with a sheet, and, with darkness falling on that ghastly scene, I fell asleep.

When I awoke, it was morning, and we were still stranded in the desert. Finally, a passerby pulled over and worked with the driver to get the Land Rover running again. Together, the men lay the corpse of the boy down the middle of the vehicle, and the rest of us all piled in around it as we made our way through the desert roads. It felt surreal and chilling to ride next to a corpse. But I had no other choice.

After many hours, we arrived at our destination: the hospital in Sebha. When I got out, somebody pointed me in the direction where I might find my parents. He offered only vague directions: "Here's the main road to get to the area where your parents are living." He told me it was about five miles from there.

On my own in this strange place, I started walking—a diminutive and sickly twelve-year-old boy, in an unfamiliar city, not knowing precisely what I was looking for. Every few minutes, another vehicle would speed toward me and each time I attempted to wave it down, each time to no avail. I felt alone, abandoned, and forlorn.

And then another person showed up. It was a man riding a rickety bicycle. He was a tall, handsome, dark-skinned man. He approached and then rode past me. My heart dropped. And then the man glanced toward me and finally stopped, turned around and approached me.

"Are you Abdulhafied!?" he asked.

"I am," I told him. "How do you know me?"

He told me his name was Aabed Mussa. He was the father of Ali Aabed, the hero who had saved the donkey from the wolf. He came from my village but had relocated years earlier to enlist in the newly established Sebha police force. As it turned out, he lived in the same suburban neighborhood as my parents. (In fact, I later learned that my parents had chosen that area in part because Aabed Mussa's family, as well as my uncle Abdullah's, were living there.)

"Hop on," he said, gesturing behind him. I climbed onto the bicycle behind Aabed Mussa and held onto his body for balance as he began pedaling down the road.

After a few miles, he stopped at a house, a simple mud structure not unlike our home in the village. There, my mother emerged, looked me over, and embraced me, surprised and delighted to see me, but shocked to find me in such poor health.

My father spent most of his time away with his work crew, rarely returning home to Sebha, so my mother was mostly alone with my brother, Abdullatif. Still getting her bearings in this new, strange place, my mother missed the familiarity of the village and her family.

Though I had been discharged from the hospital, my condition remained precarious, and my recovery was not fast in coming. For weeks and months, I lay in bed with a fever that couldn't be controlled, withering and hallucinating, sometimes fading in and out of consciousness. Once again, my mother had a mission and a purpose: to care for me and put her energies toward nursing me back to health.

Though Sebha was a much larger city than Hatiet Bergen, we were in a suburb, many miles from medical care, and with no dependable means of transportation. At one point, when I felt a slight improvement in my energy level, I asked my mother for permission to venture out to the hospital to find a cure for my fever. I set out on foot, hoping to hitch a ride. But the few cars that passed sped by, their drivers seeming to ignore me. Finally, another man on a bicycle offered me a ride. As I struggled to balance my body behind him, one of my feet became entangled in the spokes of the rear wheel, and suddenly I fell off the bike, badly injuring my leg. I never made it to the hospital, and the large gash only compounded my already difficult medical challenges.

Discouraged by my continually declining health, Mother resorted to the only other option she thought might work: spiritual healing. One night she carried me on her back to the home of an imam who had a reputation for restoring people to health. The man looked me over, placed his fingers in a cup of water, recited some verses from the Quran, and then asked me to drink the water. Next, he scrawled a few verses from the Quran on a piece of paper, folded up the page, and placed it into a small leather case, an *ihjab*, he placed around my neck, as a sort of amulet.

Putting my faith in the imam and his actions, I held on to the amulet, wearing it daily for many months. Slowly and gradually, my condition improved. Had there been real power in the Imam's words—or in the amulet? Or did my encounter with him simply lift my spirits and give me hope? I didn't know. But I was grateful to put my illness behind me.

⤜⤛⤜

I SETTLED INTO OUR NEW HOME AND WHEN SCHOOL STARTED again, I enrolled at a new school, Sebha Middle School, located about six miles from our home. I walked or rode a bicycle to get there.

Our new village in suburban Sebha was about the same size as Hatiet Bergen, the village we had come from, but its population was more diverse. Families in our home village went back generations, but this new neighborhood consisted of families from assorted tribes and ethnicities that had migrated from various parts of the country.

Some of our closest neighbors, the Tuarga family, were of Tuareg heritage, part of a large nomadic tribe that lived as far away as southern Algeria, Chad, and Mali. The Tuareg had their own distinct dialect and dress, they were known for riding camels and to being constantly on the move.

Not long after arriving, I befriended one of our Tuareg neighbors, a tall, beautiful girl named Mariam who was about three years older than I—perhaps fifteen or sixteen. In general, boys and girls didn't play together, but Mariam and I enjoyed each other's company, and we quickly grew close. Girls weren't supposed to play soccer, but she and I would routinely kick a ball around in front of her house.

During the month of Ramadan, when our families were fasting, we found ways to sneak off and enjoy food and drink together. She would tell her parents that she was taking care of her toddler brother, then the two of us would secretly help ourselves to snacks and tea away from the view of adults or other kids.

I was just entering puberty, and Mariam was considerably more developed than I. She teased me, playing a sort of cat-and-mouse game I found both alluring and confusing. Sometimes we would sleep on the floor of her house—the two of us along with five or six of her siblings. I found that exciting in ways I didn't fully understand. In time, I began to experience strong feelings, the first awakenings of my sexuality.

One night, Mariam was annoyed at her younger siblings, and repeatedly begged them to go to sleep. Ignoring her pleas, they stubbornly persisted, chattering and giggling, until we finally turned out the lanterns. As the two of us were settling down, lying on the ground, Mariam moved her head close to mine and whispered into my ear: "Make love to me."

I felt overwhelmed with excitement, but also confused and self-conscious: some of the other children were still awake next to us. Frozen and confused, I didn't act on her request (at the innocent stage, I would hardly have known how), and, somehow eventually managed to fall asleep.

In the morning, I returned home. Later that day, when I returned to Mariam's house, her mother greeted me with a stern face.

"Mariam can't play today," her mother told me. From that time on, her parents forbade her from leaving the house, and wouldn't allow us to spend time together.

A week later, I learned that Mariam was to be married. Her parents had prearranged her engagement, and the wedding would be soon.

I felt sad and forlorn. It wasn't surprising; arranged marriages were typical and expected. But I had developed warm feelings for Mariam and I longed not just for her, but for the feeling of connection the two of us enjoyed, a sensation I had not experienced before.

⸺◦◦◦⸺

I RAN INTO ANOTHER CONFLICT, THIS ONE INVOLVING AABED Musa, the man who had picked me up on his bicycle when I arrived in Sebha. He was an unusual person, just like his son Ali. Aabed was the only man I knew who managed to juggle three wives—each with several children—under one roof. The wives constantly fought with each other, competing for Aabed's attention and affection. The two older wives were from our village of Hatiet Bergen. More recently, after he moved to the Sebha area, he had married a third, a young woman we called Fezzaneia whose brother worked with my uncle. Aabed was in his late thirties when they wed, and she was fourteen or fifteen, a beautiful girl who was very likable. She was just a couple of years older than I was, and we were friendly. Being teenagers, we would chase each other around and sometimes had physical contact, though nothing serious. She once complained to Aabed that I had been physically inappropriate with her. After that, he made it clear that I wasn't welcome in his house. Still, Aabed was always kind to my family, shopping for food and staples like kerosene for us, and hauling it on his bicycle from five or ten miles away.

⸺◦◦◦⸺

DURING THE TIME WE LIVED IN SEBHA, I KEPT HEARING OF troubles back in Hatiet Bergen. The whole village erupted in a huge dispute that ended in physical altercations. For a long time, there had been jealousy and animosity between two prominent families—the Meshalish and the Gurna—over which was the leading family. The village's other families took sides, dividing the population almost equally. When the local mosque was being renovated, the dispute escalated into fist fights between the factions, with blood spilled. The behavior was so out-of-character that it caused widespread panic. Finally, some of the women called upon my Jida Gazalla to intervene. She emerged from her house, entered the mosque, and stood in the middle of the fight, begging men to listen into their hearts. Remarkably, they listened, and she successfully calmed the outrage.

CHAPTER 3

Sebha High School

———— ∞∞ ————

Two years after I moved to Sebha, my father decided to relocate the family again, this time back to Hatiet Bergen. Being away from her extended family had been difficult on my mother. She wanted to be home. I was fourteen, and it was time for me to start at the regional high school, which was in Sebha. So, when my parents and brother returned to the village, I moved into a dormitory.

Sebha High School was the single high school for the entire Fezzan region, with about four hundred students—nearly all of them boys. Girls weren't expected to pursue their education beyond the primary grades. Most of our teachers came from Egypt or Jordan. Some of them were Palestinians.

The curriculum was comprehensive and serious: world geography, world history, physics, and chemistry. We studied literature, mainly Islamic sources. They also taught us Islamic ethics and laws, but religion wasn't a dominant part of the curriculum, just one class out of many. Islam was a pervasive element of Libyan culture, so perhaps the feeling was that we didn't require much reinforcement at school.

The country was trying to advance itself, so the school emphasized subjects that were likely to propel us toward higher education. We also were also required to learn both French and English. (Students going on to study science or medicine were likely to use English; those in law or education would need French.)

My best friend at the high school was Mohammad Muftah, who was at the top of our class academically. Mohammad's father had a prominent position running the commerce and labor departments for the entire Fezzan region. More importantly to me, his family owned the local movie theater, the Sebha Cinema House, which had a large screen and a balcony. Mohammad's family lived in luxury, in a large, modern home in an exclusive Sebha neighborhood.

Though the family owned the theater, Mohammad never offered me free movie tickets, and I always held that against him. Perhaps his parents were concerned that if he did a special favor for one student, others would ask for the same treatment. In any case, Mohammad and I often went to the movies together, and I always enjoyed myself. I had grown up without television and had never seen movies, so it was a treat to watch movies so routinely. Most of the movies were American: westerns, action movies. The cinema also screened French and Indian movies. Occasionally it showed Egyptian productions, mostly propaganda films that portrayed Arabs as heroic characters and Jews as monsters.

Being around Mohammad and some of the other wealthier students sometimes brought stinging reminders of the relative poverty I came from. With a handful of other friends, we formed a small club of boys who went out each week to a movie or for a soft drink. We established a rule that we would take turns paying: each week, a different member of the club would foot the bill for the entire group. Though I agreed to the rule, I knew that I could barely afford to pay for myself, let alone the rest of the boys. I kept putting off taking my turn to pay.

Feeling cornered and not wanting to embarrass myself, I appealed for help to my Aunt Masuda, who was married to my Uncle Abdullah and lived in Sebha. I explained my predicament and told her how mortified I would be if I couldn't fulfill my obligation and pay for my friends. She seemed unconvinced, so I continued to plead my case. Still, my aunt seemed completely unmoved, not offering an ounce of sympathy—or cash.

"We have no money to give you," she finally said dismissively.

I felt even more humiliated than I had before asking her. As I left, I felt emotional pain and even nausea at my own desperation and my aunt's callous response. It was such an awful feeling that I vowed to myself that I would do my best to avoid asking for help from anyone. Particularly when it came to finances, I would find my own way in the world, relying only on myself and avoiding dependence.

During the first of my three years of high school, tensions were rising between the Arab nations and Israel, and Cairo Radio was continually broadcasting speeches by the Egyptian president, Gamal Abdel Nasser, appealing to the Arab world to rise up to liberate Palestine and drive the Jews into the Mediterranean.

I had never met a Jewish person. Though there certainly had been Jews in our area, they had long ago disappeared. Many of Libya's Jews had fled after Israel's establishment in 1948. Those that remained were concentrated in the cities of Tripoli and Benghazi, far outside of my experience. None of my textbooks had included mention of Israel. I had heard of it only as a foreign invader of Muslim land, a collaborator with Great Britain and the United States.

I knew the word *Yahudi*, Jew, only as an insult. From early childhood, the only time I had heard that word was when people would say, "Don't be a *Yahudi*." If there had ever been Jews in our area, they were invisible in my childhood, and yet adults constantly warned us not to associate with Jews. In the mosques, the imams would preach against them, describing how they had rejected the prophet and defiled the holy city of Jerusalem.

The only Jews I had ever seen were characters in the Egyptian movies I saw at Mohammad's father's theater. They were portrayed literally as monsters, hunched figures like Igor in Frankenstein movies, with bulging eyes and nasal, high-pitched voices. The movies were purely for propaganda, designed to sew anger and resentment, but I wasn't sophisticated or worldly enough to understand that.

The periodicals I saw, mostly magazines published in Egypt or Lebanon, painted a similarly sinister picture. Jews were evil killers, not to be trusted. Their aims were to accumulate power and money and to control the world, and they would do anything to achieve that purpose. No one around me questioned that view. It came from the mosques, from the media, from everyone around me. It was in the air I breathed and the water I drank.

I did know Palestinians. Of course, I had been close to O'stad Mahmood, the teacher who had moved to teach in our village. And many of the teachers at Sebha's high school were Palestinians.

Now Nasser, a powerful and charismatic speaker, delivered speeches every week—sometimes more often—imploring all Arabs to slaughter the Jews. In June of 1967, toward the end of my first high-school year, those calls reached a fevered pitch. On the morning of June 6, I was in the dormitory when my cousin Madani, who was two years ahead of me in school, got my attention. (Madani was the same cousin who had helped with writing the poem about my father's enemy back in the village.)

"Abdulhafied, do you know what's happening in Palestine?" I was only vaguely aware of the situation, as I wasn't yet in the habit of following the news as he was. Madani explained to me that the Israeli air force had attacked Egypt. Now the entire Arab world was rising up to destroy the Jews. The Egyptians had already retaliated, he said, and now the Jordanians and Iraqis were joining in to finish the task.

"Come," he implored me, "we've got to do something."

From birth, we had been raised to hate Jews, and now it was time to take action. I felt an almost physical need to release my anger. But what could we do in our small corner of the world to help the cause of liberating Palestine? Here in Sebha, we didn't have any Jews to throw into the sea.

Without hesitating, I followed my cousin. We made our way to Sebha's downtown area, where the police headquarters and other government offices were. There, a crowd was gathering outside the area's only Western-style establishment, a bar. In our entirely Muslim country, alcohol was forbidden. But we knew this pub was frequented by Americans and other foreigners. I had ridden by the bar many times on my way to my middle school, often spotting discarded beer bottles in the street or on the outskirts of the city, where foreigners would be drinking at night and leave behind empty glass bottles.

Madani and I joined the angry, boisterous crowd, and I found myself shouting chants along with everyone else: "Death to the Jews!" "Throw the Jews into the Sea!" "Liberate Palestine!"

It was midday. The pub was closed and nobody was inside. Finally, some of the older teenagers broke down the door. Storming into the building, they grabbed every bottle they could reach, carried them outside, and dumped the contents into the street. Standing in the hot sun, we continued chanting amidst the odor of beer, wine, and liquor on the pavement and in the soaked soil.

The chanting went on for at least an hour: "Death to the Jews!"

Of course, we hadn't accomplished anything. We hadn't changed the situation or contributed to the war effort. All we had done was empty some bottles and vent our teenage energy. But I felt a sense of release, a feeling of being part of something larger than myself.

As it turned out, we had been operating on false information. Later that week, we learned what had actually happened—or at least a different version of events. At a relative's home in Sebha, men and boys gathered around a radio to listen to Gamal Abdel Nasser, the Egyptian president, deliver a speech. He called what had happened a *neksa*, a significant setback for the Arab world. He took full responsibility and apologized for his failures. He announced that he would resign and withdraw from public life.

Of course, the Arab world was having none of that. By the millions, people took to the streets to protest, insisting that he stay in power. A master politician, he had seized the moment to solidify his power.

THE DAY-TO-DAY DRAMAS OF HIGH SCHOOL MAY HAVE BEEN considerably less gripping than what was happening on the political stage, but to me, they felt no less important. In my second year of high school, one of the most significant events was something called Science Day. It was a much-anticipated occasion when regular classes were canceled and parents and local residents would flock to the school to observe the proceedings. Some students created displays to exhibit physics or chemistry experiments they had performed. The most prestigious part, though, was the science quiz. Each year, the administrators and teachers would select a small number of students from each grade to compete in the quiz. Given all of that attention, there was intense competition among the students to be selected to represent the grade.

I was sitting in science class one day when an administrator showed up at the door and told us that he had news to share. "We have chosen your class representatives for the Science Day quiz," he said. The room grew silent as we waited eagerly, each hoping to hear our own name. Then it came: "Your representatives will be Mohammad Muftah... and Abdulhafied Elhaderi."

That moment changed me. For the first time, I felt recognized for my mind and for my hard work. I was being acknowledged as one of the academic leaders of my class. My teachers had recognized me. Mohammad and I were already close friends, but this designation gave us a new connection—as well as a mission. We immediately got to work studying the subjects that would be covered in the quiz. For many weeks, the two of us drilled each other, eager to show our scientific prowess. We did well in the competition, but the important thing was that I had been chosen. I felt a sense of pride and excitement. I was somebody.

ALL OF THE STUDENTS AT THE HIGH SCHOOL WERE MALE, WITH a few exceptions: three girls who were the daughters of teachers. Two were the daughters of teachers who were Palestinians, and one was the daughter of a Libyan teacher. The girls in my village were allowed in school only through fifth grade so they would not be considered graduates of elementary school. After that, their expected role in life was to prepare themselves for marriage.

At the high school, the few girls in our classes sat in the back rows of classrooms, and we boys were instructed not to interact with them—or even look at them or call them by name. None of us questioned those practices. It was just the way things were. The school was heavily influenced by Islam, with its particular gender roles, and by the tribal cultures of our region.

During high school, I lived in a dormitory with about two hundred boys from all over the region. Each hallway housed the boys from a different region of the Fezzan. Every hall had about twenty boys, sleeping in bunk beds.

THE SCHOOL DIDN'T EMPHASIZE RELIGIOUS PRACTICE, BUT THE education was infused with a strong dose of nationalism. Every morning, we were required to line up and listen to the Libyan national anthem, followed by speeches extolling the strength and importance of the kingdom. It was the mid-1960s, a time of heightened tensions in the Middle East, particularly between Israel and its Arab neighbors.

Sebha was far more connected to the outside world than the village. We had access to European newspapers and radio broadcasts as well as American magazines such as *Time* and *Newsweek*. We even knew about the Beatles. I had never heard their music, but everyone knew about them. On a visit back to my village, even a Bedouin camel herder mentioned the Beatles. A classmate told me about a dance called the Twist. Somehow, these bits of popular culture from outside our realm seeped into our reality. They were in the air.

While I was in high school, I discovered a very special building in Sebha, a modern, white, one-story structure built on the main street. It was built around a courtyard with a fountain and flowerbeds. It was the city's American Center.

After World War II, Libya was divided into three regions. The Americans administered the Northern region, where Tripoli was; the British administered the Eastern section, where Benghazi was located; and the French oversaw the southern region, where I lived. But after Libya gained its independence in 1951, the U.S. extended its influence to the southern region.

This building served as the residence for the Fezzan region's U.S. consulate.

Entering the building, what first caught my attention was a large portrait of President Kennedy, smiling and youthful. The front section of the building housed a large library that was open to the public. During high school, I spent many afternoons there, reading the newspapers and magazines— in both Arabic and English—and enjoying the luxury of air conditioning, the first I had ever experienced. (In Sebha, not even the hospital was air-conditioned.)

I read American comic strips, thumbed through American newspapers, and also enjoyed access to a bounty of materials printed in Arabic. Earlier in life, what I had known of America was that it was the faraway place that sent food and shoes and blankets to our village by way of the CARE truck. I would later learn that Libya had close ties to the United States dating back to beginnings of American history. President George Washington initiated the Treaty of Tripoli (see "Treaty of Tripoli"on page 176), which was signed by President John Adams in 1796 to secure shipping rights to American ships in the Mediterranean and protect them from pirates. The phrase "the shores of Tripoli" in the U.S. Marines' hymn refers to the first time the American flag was hoisted in the Old World, in 1805 by Marines during the Battle of Derna, during the Barbary War. (Derna is just east of Benghazi, on the Mediterranean). Later, it was the guidance and generosity of Americans that helped sustain Libyans in the 1950s and the 1960s. Armand Hammer of Occidental Petroleum discovered oil in Libya in the 1960s, propelling the new nation to become an affluent and important strategic force in North Africa. Wheelus Air Base, in Tripoli, home to America's Sixth Fleet in the 1960s, was once America's largest military facility outside the U.S., with its own shopping mall, post office, high school, television and radio stations, and a population over 10,000.

While I might have learned some of that as a high school student in Sebha, it was spending time in the American Center, this well-appointed, welcoming, and comfortable place, that helped to strengthen my fondness for America and all it stood for even more.

AFTER MY SECOND YEAR OF HIGH SCHOOL, I SPENT THE SUMMER
with my family, then living back in the village of Hatiet
Bergen. Feeling stuck and bored in the tiny community, I felt
eager to explore beyond the world with which I was already
familiar. I begged my father to let me make a trip to Tripoli,
explaining that I wanted to spend time with some relatives
there. I finally nagged him enough to agree to pay, and I set
off, planning to stay for three weeks. I wasn't sure where
I would stay, but my Uncle Mashri dictated a letter to me
to present to his wife's brother, Tahir Ibarhim, who was an
army officer living there.

Tagging along with a few adults from the village, I hitched
a ride to Sebha, where I purchased a bus ticket for Tripoli.
The bus left mid-day and drove into the night. I was so
excited that I could barely sleep.

When I awoke the next morning, we were nearing Tripoli. I was filled with excitement. Almost everything was
eye-opening and exciting: the paved streets, the multitude
of cars, the traffic lights. I gazed at the buildings as high as
five stories tall—far beyond any structure I had seen. Then
the Mediterranean Sea came into view, with its deep blue
waters. The place was full of life. Instead of one movie theater, there were half a dozen. I saw bakeries and cafes and
cafeterias. Tripoli felt like an enchanted land.

Arriving at the bus station, I found my way to the Foundug Alhouria (Arabic for Liberty Motel), where about twenty
other people from our village were staying, crammed into a
tiny motel room. Each room in the hotel housed people from
a different village who had reason to be in Tripoli, either
temporarily or on a longer-term basis. The quarters were
terribly cramped, with all of those people sharing a single
toilet and a single faucet. Some of the residents had been

living in those conditions for years, yet everyone seemed to live in harmony, relatively free of conflict. People from the various villages intermingled freely, often exchanging favors or cooperating to prepare meals.

After a few days, my cousin Tahir came to the hotel to retrieve me. I showed him the letter Uncle Mashri had dictated, and he brought me to his home in a Tripoli suburb, near the university.

Every day in Tripoli was filled with novel experiences, sights, and sounds that surprised and delighted me. I saw television for the first time. I felt the cool Mediterranean breeze on my face. I ate fresh fish. Some days I packed in two or three different movie screenings. I bathed regularly in the only Turkish bath in Tripoli, which was located in the old Jewish quarter, known as Hara.

I also witnessed an underside of life I hadn't previously experienced: I learned that some of the village men with whom I shared the hotel room paid regular visits to a nearby brothel. Libya may have been a Muslim country, with all of the prohibitions and religious laws that implied, but prostitution finds ways to thrive practically anywhere.

ALONG WITH THE ACADEMIC LEARNING I DID IN HIGH SCHOOL, I also gained some major life lessons, some of them difficult and painful.

For the most part, I had been fortunate that, despite our difficult living conditions, most of my closest friends had survived childhood more or less intact. The one tragic exception was one of the people closest to me, Sharif Abuejuela, a cousin on my father's side of the family who was a year older and a promising student. (Sharif was the one who helped circulate the poem Madani and I wrote after my father's fight.) During his first year in middle school in Brak, Sharif went with some friends to a mountain called Abu Shekshaska, on the outskirts of Brak. It was known as forbidden territory because large amounts of explosives and military equipment left over from World War II had been stored there, dangerously left there with the full knowledge of local residents and the government.

When Sharif and his friends arrived at the site, they innocently started playing with the piles of stuff they discovered there, including grenades and other devices. Even when they heard noises coming from explosives, they apparently didn't realize the risk they were taking, so they kept playing until they set off a catastrophic explosion. It shattered their young bodies. Of the ten friends, six died on the scene—including my cousin. The other four suffered serious injuries.

I was in the village the next day when a police vehicle arrived with Sharif's body. Devastated, his older brothers prepared him for burial on a farm outside the village, protecting their mother from having to see his shattered body. Then they buried my friend and cousin at the village cemetery. I felt sad, unable to make sense of the loss.

The early encounter with tragedy did little to prepare me for some of the setbacks that befell other people close to me, such as my high school classmate Kailani. Though I was never athletic—because of my frail health in childhood as well as my small stature and poor nutrition—I always admired my classmates who excelled in sports. One of them was Kailani, who was tall, strong, and handsome. Sebha had a local soccer league with a handful of teams, and one of them chose him for its roster. He became one of the team's stars, performing before large cheering crowds. A combination of his athletic prowess and his good nature made him one of the most popular and beloved members of our class.

But social status didn't give Kailani immunity to occasional challenges. Our physics class was taught by one of my favorite teachers, O'stad Mustafa, a large bear of a man who came from Syria and had a reputation as a popular and compassionate educator. One morning during a physics lab, O'Stad Mustafa was pouring fluid into a longneck flask when, as the air escaped, it emitted an amusing whistle sound. Hearing it, we all instinctively burst out in loud laughter, Kailani chuckling a bit more loudly than the rest of us. For reasons I didn't understand, Kailani's laughter angered the teacher, who immediately confronted him and asked Kailani to stand up. Kailani complied, rising to his full height—nearly as tall as the teacher.

"Do you want to tell me why you were laughing?" O'Stad Mustafa demanded, suddenly no longer the cool, easygoing teacher I had so admired.

Taken aback, Kailani tried to explain: "It just sounded funny."

Not amused, O'stad Mustafa abruptly lifted his hand and slapped Kailani across the face—with such force that Kailani, shocked, began to weep. Without another word, the teacher stormed out of the classroom, leaving us all in stunned silence, as Kailani pulled out a handkerchief to shield his face and wipe away the tears. I sat at my desk in disbelief, trying to make sense of the uncharacteristic act of cruelty.

Sadly, it was far from the worst thing that happened to Kailani during high school. Later that same school year, he was playing in the final game of the soccer league championship when he took a kick to the head and collapsed on the field. He remained unconscious for some time, lapsing into a coma in Sebha Central Hospital. When he didn't recover, they sent him on the once-weekly airplane flight from Sebha to Tripoli, where he was hospitalized.

Kailani was never the same again. Of all of my contemporaries, he had seemed among the most certain to enjoy a life of great accomplishment and success. After five years on the soccer team, he had been playing in his final game, and one moment had changed his life's course forever. Later in high school, he returned, but he was physically diminished, a shadow of the strong, confident, and skilled athlete I had once known. The aura of physicality he had once projected was gone.

Unfortunately, Kailani wasn't my only classmate to encounter a random and heartbreaking setback. Idris was another a star athlete, the son of the chief of the Sebha area's military brigade. His family was well off, and Idris lived next door to my friend Mohammed, whose family owned the cinema. One morning, Idris didn't show up to school. It didn't seem alarming, but none of us knew why he wasn't there. The next day, we found out: Idris's father had been driving his luxury Mercedes Benz in the northeast of the country when he'd been killed in an awful traffic accident. Idris never returned to school: the entire family relocated to the north to be close to relatives.

Each time I saw a classmate experience such a calamity, I felt empathy and I was also struck by how unfair and unpredictable life could be. It was particularly striking that these two fellow students whom I had so admired to the point of jealousy were not protected by their status or talents. Sometimes life just wasn't fair.

I hardly knew how to process those kinds of tragedies. From an early age, I had a strong, rational mind. Using reason to make sense of events was one way of surviving. When a situation seemed inexplicable or made me uncomfortable, I tended to ignore it, pushing it from my consciousness or trying to convince myself that I actually did not need to understand it.

That was how I reacted to my own confrontation with one of my educators, a Palestinian-born English teacher who was physically imposing and had a grim face adorned with a bushy mustache. When students made mistakes, he humiliated them—or even slapped them. I found his presence to be so intimidating that whenever he called on me to read or speak in class, I experienced a terrible stutter. My stuttering lasted for months and caused me even more anxiety. But I didn't share my angst with anyone else. Instead, I assured myself that it was the teacher's fault and that the stutter was limited to that one teacher's classroom. (That turned out to be true.)

IN OUR FINAL YEAR OF HIGH SCHOOL CAME THE NATIONAL Scholastic Exam, a test required of every high school student in Libya to help determine whether we might be eligible to continue our studies in university. The school administered the exams over an entire week and they were comprehensive, covering about ten academic subjects.

The exams arrived at our school in a package sent from Tripoli. Our administrators treated them with the utmost care and attention to security. The envelope for each subject test was sealed with wax to thwart any kind of cheating, and nobody was allowed to open the packet until it was time to start each exam. In the rooms where we took the exams, proctors directed us to sit far apart to prevent us from copying or collaborating.

All of these factors combined to give the testing period a certain feeling of gravitas. We all sensed that how we performed on these exams would determine the direction of our lives. They would serve to sort us, and there was a definite bias toward the sciences. Libya in the 1960s was a poor country that needed more scientists and doctors to help it advance in the world. Those who scored in the top tier would go into medicine; the second tier, engineering; the third, physics; and the lowest, education or law. The University of Tripoli was known for its science departments; the University of Benghazi was more focused on the humanities, law, and economics. So, the exam also was likely to determine where we spent our university years and what opportunities were available to us in the future. An older cousin gave me his favorite fountain pen as a gift and as a gesture of good luck. That act of generosity and moral support provided inspiration to put in my best effort.

We took the exams in the early summer, at the same time as students throughout the country. Then came the wait to see how we scored. To maintain fairness in grading, the schools sent exams to Tripoli, where workers in a central office graded every examination in the country. The news of the results arrived in dramatic form: a radio announcer read them on the air following the evening newscast over several nights. The announcements came in order: first results from the Tripoli region, followed by other regions, including, eventually, our own Fezzan region. Everyone tuned live in to hear the voice on the radio read the name of the student, followed by the news of which tier you scored in.

Or almost everyone. Since the school year had ended, I

had returned for the summer to the village, and there was no radio available. I knew when the announcement was due, but rather than receiving the news directly, I had to wait until a distant cousin made a trip to Sebha and checked with the education department for me. He woke me up one morning with good news: I had scored in the second tier. I was going to the University of Tripoli!

My hard work had paid off. I felt excited about my future and the possibilities ahead of me, thrilled at the prospect of living in the city I had eagerly explored the previous summer.

A part of me also felt pride of accomplishment. Since early childhood, people had compared me to my cousin Madani, who was two years older and had a reputation as the smartest kid to emerge from our village. Though I looked up to Madani, I was also jealous of him. Because he was older, he was considered to be wiser. But I knew that when Madani took the exam, his score had placed him only in the third tier. At last, I had proven myself; I had outperformed my rival.

I spent the next few weeks in the village preparing to head off to university, and also taking care of my mother, whose health had been in sharp decline. She was suffering from a debilitating lung disease that caused a chronic and frequent cough, her vision was failing, and she was so weak that she had come to spend much of her time at home in bed.

Mostly, though, I was focused on the future. My plan was to travel by Land Rover to Sebha and then to catch a bus to Tripoli. On the evening I was preparing to leave, Mother called me to come to her side. The truck waited outside to take me from the village, but she insisted that I linger for a few moments before I ran off.

"This could be the last time I see you," she said, embracing me. It hadn't crossed my mind that her illness was severe enough to be life-threatening. I assured her that we'd be together soon when I came back from my first year. I gave her a last hug, then hurried to the Land Rover, which took me to Sebha.

There, I met Mailud El Arabi, my classmate with whom I'd had a competitive, love-hate relationship for most of high school, and the two of us boarded a bus for Tripoli.

CHAPTER 4

Grief and Growth in Tripoli

⌒⌒⌒

We arrived about a week before classes started. That gave us gave us time to get acclimated to our new surroundings. Another high school friend a couple of years our senior showed us around the campus. He took us to the administrative offices, where we arranged for housing and some of the basics of student life: linens, dining-hall passes, and the like.

I enrolled in the engineering program, taking the cluster of introductory courses required for every first-year engineering student.

⌒⌒⌒

MY FIRST YEAR OF COLLEGE COINCIDED WITH A PERIOD OF DRA-matic political change that was sweeping Libyan society. In September of that year, a few months before I arrived in Tripoli, Col. Muammar Gaddafi staged a coup and rose to power.

In his effort to cement his regime he played to the public, promising higher wages for workers and whatever else it took to win their support. He also enlisted students in his efforts. On many weekends during my first year at university, I joined groups of students who piled onto large buses that transported us to fruit-tree groves, where we lent our hands in harvesting crops—oranges, lemons, olives. We weren't paid for our work, but I felt like I was performing a civic duty, doing my part to help the country at an important moment.

At the time, I viewed Gaddafi as a positive force. After all, at a time when the rest of the Arab world was moving toward becoming more modern and secular, he had toppled the Libyan monarchy. He promised to liberalize Libyan society, promote freedom of expression, and defeat Israel.

But there were signs from the beginning that Gaddafi wouldn't be entirely benign. Following that September, he cracked down on anyone who was known to be Islamist or communist, rounding up "suspects" and throwing them in jail. That included some outspoken students at the university. But the country was so swept up in the euphoria of a new regime that most people paid little attention to those less pleasant aspects of the change. Gaddafi spoke so eloquently and vociferously about freedom of speech and freedom of assembly that many seemed to overlook what was actually happening.

As for me, I was determined to keep my head down and focus on my schoolwork. My objective was to do as well as I could in my academic work and, in the process, figure out my next steps in life.

<hr />

ONE DAY NEAR THE END OF THAT FIRST YEAR, AROUND JULY OF 1970, I was sitting in class when a staffer from the school office arrived at the door and called me to the administrative offices. When I arrived, I found sitting there the last person I ever expected to see in a university office: my father. He seemed terribly out of place in that academic setting. Spotting me, he immediately jumped from his chair, and, without speaking, opened his arms and embraced me. I knew there was something wrong. Surely there had been a death – my mother? Or maybe my brother?

He didn't tell me in words. He simply gestured for me to come with him, and we walked out of the office together, and without speaking, continued for twenty minutes to a bus stop. There, we boarded a bus that took us to the downtown area, where my father was staying at Foundug Alhouria, the same motel where I had stayed during my summer visit nearly two years earlier. Even without words, I understood what he had come to tell me: we had lost my mother. I felt an overwhelming sadness.

My father was a quiet man. He simply didn't know how to break the awful news to me. Despite our strained relationship and the distance between us, I was grateful that he had made the journey. It would have been easier for him to ask someone else to break the news of my mother's death. He had obviously hurried to get to me in Tripoli. He hadn't even packed clothing for the journey, though it was wintertime. In that moment, I felt his love and caring. I didn't feel alone.

I stayed overnight at the hotel, comforted to be surrounded by others from our village. The next morning, I thanked my father, said goodbye, and made my way back to the dormitory.

Only sometime later did I learn what had befallen my mother: she had grown so ill that her family urged my father to take her from the village to the hospital in Sebha. He caught a ride on the only accessible Land Rover, paying a steep price. But ultimately he had acted too late. In the middle of the night, a few hours out of Hatiet Bergen, my mother had stopped breathing. There, in the middle of the desert, she died.

Bereft, my father had worked with the driver to fill the truck-bed with sand and laid her body on it, using the sand to prevent the body from bouncing as the vehicle traversed the rough desert roadways.

Five or six hours after they had left the village, they returned, and, seeing the vehicle, the neighbors and friends knew immediately what had happened.

Though I was full of sadness, I chose not to share the news of my mother's death with any classmates. I kept it inside. We were approaching our final exams, and I opted to pour all of my grief into my studies. For two weeks, I became focused in a way I had never previously experienced. I felt as if I was in a bubble, with nothing to distract me from my studies.

I was like a different person. Nobody offered guidance or counseling to cope with my grief; that simply wasn't a part of Libyan culture. I felt more than ever before that I was responsible for my own destiny. I directed my energies toward my schoolwork. That was my way of coping.

Perhaps my reaction was informed by my experiences as a child in the village, where death was all around me and it was common to see women and entire families wailing and throwing sand in the air as raw and open expressions of grief. It was common to see the body of a child or infant carried on a platform for burial. Accustomed to such uncontrollable grief, perhaps I wanted to exert some control, to grieve in the manner I preferred, and not in such a dramatic and public way.

MY SINGULAR FOCUS PAID OFF IN WAYS I COULD NOT HAVE imagined. When the department announced the grades, I learned that I had scored among the top five students. My classmates were shocked. Many of them came from bigger cities and larger high schools that had offered them far more academic preparation than I had received in Sebha. Surely my instructors and classmates alike began to wonder: who is this kid from a little village in the south who is suddenly an academic star?

The truth was that I was as shocked by the results as my classmates were. I had always been a proficient student, but certainly not an exceptional one. If my mother hadn't died just then, if I hadn't channeled my grief in that way I did, if her death had caused me to fall apart instead of increasing my focus, I might have settled in as just another mediocre student. Instead, her death propelled me to new levels of achievement.

That experience changed me. I was filled with pride and a new sense of self-confidence. It also opened doors. Scoring at that level meant that I could have my choice of a profession. Within the engineering department, the university offered five sub-specialties: electrical, mechanical, civil, architectural, and chemical engineering. I briefly considered the idea of opting for the architecture program, because I knew that department had the most female students and I liked the idea of studying among women. But in the end, I opted for the program that seemed to hold the most promise, chemical engineering.

The chemical engineering major was a new option. A big part of Gaddafi's plan was to nationalize the emerging petroleum and petrochemical industries. I was the first student to enroll as a chemical engineering major.

From early on in my university education, I set a goal to pursue my graduate studies abroad. It was common for the best students to go on government-sponsored scholarships to study in Russia, in Europe or—for the best students—in the United States. Since my high-school days, when I happened upon the American Center in Sebha, I had dreamed about traveling to the United States. Now I became more determined than ever to achieve that. The prospect of studying at an American university gave me reason to work hard to maintain my place at the top of the two dozen students in our academically rigorous department.

SINCE I WAS PREPARING FOR A CAREER IN THE OIL INDUSTRY, I spent every college summer working in the industry, either in the desert oil fields or at a facility on the Mediterranean Sea where Esso—the American corporation that was a precursor to Exxon—refined and shipped petroleum. Each facility had two separate areas, one for the staff of mostly Americans who oversaw various aspects of the operations, and one for the mostly Libyan employees, the blue-collar workers who did the hands-on work of running the facilities.

As students, we were housed in the American part of the compound, which was fully equipped to serve the American workers and their families. The largest base at Mersa Brega, an expansive complex on the Mediterranean, included restaurants, a cinema, and even a bowling alley. The first time I walked into the cafeteria for breakfast I was so overwhelmed that my jaw dropped. I simply couldn't believe the expansive selection of food: multiple varieties of juice (apple, grape, orange, grapefruit) and a full menu of entrees, including pancakes, omelets, scrambled eggs, various fruits, breads, and more. I had grown up hoping for scraps from the CARE truck, so it was overwhelming to come upon this remarkable spread, all plentiful and readily available. (It was also my introduction to an ingenious product I would come to love: peanut butter.)

Lunch was even more breathtaking: chicken, beef, French fries, various pasta and rice dishes, and cake and ice cream for dessert. I couldn't believe my eyes.

My English was limited, but I tried to ask one of the American workers how the company could possibly offer such a striking selection of foods.

"This is nothing," he said. "You could walk into a cafeteria in any small town in the United States and find the same thing."

The food was one thing. Then we got to experience bowling. The shiny wood floors! White pins lined up in neat rows! If I already felt an attraction to America, now it became a preoccupation. I felt more motivated to get myself to this place where everything was in such abundance and so full of fun—such a contrast to the village of my origin. (And I never dined at the facility that served Libyan-style food to the Libyan workers. Why bother?)

The job offered exposure to a variety of the types of work required at the facilities that pump and refine petroleum. I often worked with another student under the direction of an American technician. Together, we would drive through the oil fields taking various measurements— pressure, temperature, fluid levels—to monitor the operations and then alert technicians when they needed to call service workers to make repairs or adjustments. Oil production is a highly technical field and this on-the-job experience helped me learn the various technical aspects of oil excavation and processing.

THE SUMMER JOB ALSO LED TO AN UNPLEASANT CONFLICT WITH my father. I spent the summer after my second year of college at Esso's desert oil production facility and earned about one hundred and fifty dinars, the equivalent of five months of my father's salary as a road-crew supervisor. I never told my father how much I was earning, but sometime after the summer ended, a cousin got in touch with me to tell me that my father wanted to have a share of my summer's earnings.

I found his request infuriating. I had worked hard to earn that money, and if my father wanted some of it, I felt that he should have made the request directly to me instead of making the appeal indirectly, through a relative. I decided that I needed to confront him. During a break toward the end of that summer, I spent some time back in the village. One evening I had dinner at home with my father—just the two of us, under the dim lights of a kerosene lantern.

I told my father how angry it made me that he had resorted to going through my cousin to ask for my money. "If you want something from me," I told him forcefully, "You need to ask me directly." Besides, I said, I would be keeping that money to help cover my college expenses.

He didn't utter a word in reply, just kept puffing on his hand-rolled cigarette. Afterward, I felt some relief that I had expressed my feelings, however difficult the encounter had been. And I had the sense that, in a way, he was pleased that

I had stood up for myself. That evening, I gained a share of my father's respect.

THE SUMMER AFTER MY SECOND YEAR AT THE UNIVERSITY, THREE friends and I traveled by taxi to Egypt. We journeyed along the Mediterranean Highway, stopping at a number of major cities: Sirte, Benghazi, Derna, and Tobruk in Libya, and in Egypt, El Alamein, Alexandria, and finally Cairo. At the time, Cairo was the Arab world's prime destination, and we spent ten wild days and nights there, in awe of the city's entertainment and culture: night clubs with live music, wonderful museums, restaurants and shops on the Nile River, and live theater featuring the best-known actors and comedians. We even visited the Great Pyramids and the Sphinx.

That trip was also the first time any of us had partaken in alcohol or cigarettes. That alone made it a memorable vacation. We were enjoying ourselves so much that we stayed longer than we could afford, even spending last dinars we had allocated for the taxi fare home. After a few days diligently searching at downtown Cairos's Libyan taxi terminal, we somehow managed to find an unusually understanding taxi driver who was willing to drive us with the understanding that we would pay him when we arrived back at Tripoli. He probably felt sorry for the four of us, young Libyan men stranded and broke in Egypt. We weren't the first Libyan tourists to suffer that fate.

I visited Cairo two more times during college. Once I went by bus on a school trip to see Egypt's petro-chemical infrastructure. On that trip we also traveled within Egypt by plane to visit the Aswan Dam, the Karnack and

Luxor Temples, and the Valley of Kings—where numerous tombs of pharaohs were located. We also spent a day on an ancient sailboat on the Nile. I made my third trip by plane when I was a college teaching assistant, with plenty of money to spend.

DURING THE SCHOOL YEAR, I WAS QUITE ATTENTIVE TO MY STUDies. Not that I had a lot of alternatives to studying. There were female students, but, as in high school, the administration discouraged the male students from interacting with them. In any case, most of the young women were from upper-class Tripoli society—they drove their own cars or had drivers—so they likely wouldn't have interacted with someone of my impoverished background.

Beyond studies, the university didn't offer many extracurricular activities. Once a week or so I would take a bus downtown to see a movie or wash my clothes at a laundromat. As for religion, everyone in Libya was Sunni Muslim, but the university didn't have a mosque or any kind of prayer or religious study group. Religious practice simply wasn't a central part of my life.

My penchant for using words to describe events or people occasionally got me into trouble in college. One of my professors was a heavyset man who always wore a white coat and loved to write on the blackboard with colored chalk. In his oversized coat, he looked like a cartoon character. I gave him a nickname: Professor Sh'kara, meaning Professor Barley Sack. The name stuck, and became so popular with students that at one official meeting, a student inadvertently referred to him by nickname instead of his real name. When someone asked who the student was talking about, some of my classmates turned knowingly toward me. It was all in good fun, but I was grateful that the moment passed without anyone exposing me as the smart aleck.

As my final project as an undergraduate, I was assigned to design an oil production facility. The department assigned me certain parameters: how many barrels per day would be produced, what type of fuel it would be producing, and various other details. I had four months to design a theoretical facility from beginning to end.

MY HARD WORK PAID OFF. OVER THE FIVE YEARS OF COLLEGE required in the engineering programs, I maintained my grades and kept my position as the university's top chemical engineering student. The department was highly competitive, and there were certainly other students trying to outperform me, but none succeeded. At graduation, my work was recognized. I was awarded the First Honor National Academic Award, which honored students who maintained excellent grades and top class-rankings throughout their college careers. I was the first person from the Fezzan region to earn such a prestigious national award, and winning gave me recognition throughout the country (to the chagrin of some of my more competitive peers).

I was invited to a ceremony where Libya's prime minister, Abdessalam Jalloud, was to present me the award. Ironically, by then my university funding had run out, and I was low on cash. At the time, I owned only one decent shirt and one presentable pair of pants. I would wash them at night and hang them out to dry while I slept, then put on the same clothes again in the morning. Those were the clothes I wore to the ceremony where I shook the hand of the Libyan prime minister.

Despite the prestige it supposedly represented, the honor didn't help me land a job immediately. The university offered practically no help in that area. It simply wasn't equipped to connect students with jobs. Finally, though, I landed a job as a teaching assistant at the university. It came with a good salary and housing in a dormitory, so during that academic year, I could finally afford to splurge a bit on clothing and managed to put a significant amount into savings.

I was still determined to pursue my education outside of Libya, so during that year I also sought the advice of three of my favorite professors in the department about how and where to pursue my graduate education in the United States. They directed me to the three chemical engineering programs they said had the best reputations: the University of Wisconsin–Madison, MIT, and UC Berkeley. I sent off applications to all three, taking my professors' word and not bothering to do any of my own research about the universities—their culture, their locations, their climates.

One thing I didn't worry about was paying tuition. The country would be footing the entire bill and also paying me a generous monthly stipend for living expenses. Libya was investing in me with the expectation that I would return and teach in a university. It was all part of Gaddafi's mission to transform Libya into a strong and self-sufficient nation. It was hardly a "no-strings-attached" deal. I was required to sign what seemed to be hundreds of documents, promising that in accepting the scholarship I agreed to return to the country. I didn't give it much thought. I assumed that was what I would eventually do, but at the time, I was mostly focused on my studies and the adventures ahead.

As it turned out, all three American universities offered me admission (not surprisingly, since the Libyan government would be footing the bill for my tuition and all expenses). I opted for the top-ranked program, Wisconsin.

*Ed Elhaderi, center, with high school classmates at
Sebha High School, 1969.*

Ed's father, Elsaidi Elhaderi, wearing traditional Libyan jarid in his 1972 passport photo for hajj *to Mecca.*

*Ed Elhaderi, right, receiving the prestigeous First National Honor
Award in Engineering from the then Prime Minister of Libya,
Abdessalam Jalloud, of Gaddafi's Government, July 1974.*

*Ed's father, Elsaidi Elhaderi, at the entrance to his home
in Hatiet Bergen, Libya, 1979.*

Barbara and Ed Elhaderi, on their first date, 1979.

Ed Elhaderi's self-portrait in pencil, 1980.

Ed and Barbara Elhaderi's wedding, December 26, 1980.

Ed Elhaderi, PhD, with Barbara at U.S.C. commencement, 1982.

Ed and Barbara celebrate Ed's American citizenship, 1985.

Barbara and Ed Elhaderi on their first cruise to the Carribean, 1988.

Ed and Barbara's son, Jason, becoming a bar mitzvah, at the Russian Chabad Synagogue, West Hollywood, California, 2006.

Jason Elhaderi's bar mitzvah. Left to right: Jessica Elhaderi, sister; Ellen Levin, grandmother; Robert Levin, grandfather; Jason Elhaderi; Barbara Elhaderi, mom; Ed Elhaderi, dad, 2006.

Ed, Barbara, Jessica, and Jason, Surfing Goat Dairy, Maui, 2008.

Ed, Jason, and Jessica during a visit to Jason
at U.C. Santa Cruz, 2014.

CHAPTER 5

Discovering America:
A Dream Come True

⌖

In the summer of 1975, I packed my suitcase and headed for America. My first flight was from Tripoli to Zurich. Looking through the airplane window at Switzerland, I caught my first glimpse of Europe, taking in a green and lush landscape that looked nothing like the arid deserts of Libya. Not only did everything look different, but I felt different. I had a sense of freedom and possibility. I was finally on my own, beginning a new life. My future was in my own hands.

I had put considerable deliberation into this new adventure. My decision to open a new chapter in the United States was in stark contrast with the choices of most of my Libyan colleagues, who were marrying and settling down in Libya. They saw clinging to the culture they knew as the surest antidote to what they saw happening in America of the 1970s: racial unrest, progressive liberalism, the political upheavals triggered by the Vietnam War and Watergate.

From Zurich, I flew to Washington, D.C., and after a brief layover, I boarded an Ozark Airlines flight to Champaign-Urbana, Illinois, where I spent my first three months in America in an English language program at the University of Illinois Champaign-Urbana.

As I learned the language, I also acclimated to life in America. I listened to country music for the first time and the radio constantly played the sweet and innocent songs of John Denver, which touched my heart. At the time, there wasn't much in town besides the university. What made the biggest impression was a restaurant, McDonald's. On my first visit to McDonald's, I ordered a Big Mac and fries. The hamburger was so large that I ate just a few bites. It seemed like so much food! I couldn't imagine how one person could sit down and eat an entire Big Mac and French fries in a single sitting.

In Champaign-Urbana, I also purchased my first car, spending my stipend on a bright red Chevrolet Vega. I had very little experience behind the wheel. In Tripoli, I had taken a few driving lessons, but I never earned a license. Somehow, that didn't matter.

That summer I visited the local Department of Motor Vehicles to obtain my driver's license. With luck, I passed both the written exam and the behind-the-wheel test. As the clerk gathered my information for the license, he asked for my birth date.

"Nineteen fifty-one," I told him.

"Well, how about the day and the month?" he asked, annoyed. I told him I didn't have a birth date—that no one had asked before. Amused, he politely explained that if I wanted to obtain a license, I'd need a birth date. I had to choose one month out of twelve and one day out of thirty. I settled on September 1.

License in hand, I was able to drive legally. That November, I drove to Madison, Wisconsin, to start my new life as a graduate student.

For months, I had been eagerly anticipating this next chapter in my life and education, but my arrival in Madison didn't exactly go as scripted. I pulled into town around midnight. Tired and unfamiliar with the area or with American road signs, I soon heard a siren and saw a flashing light behind me. I pulled over, and a police officer approached me, sternly telling me that I had been driving the wrong way on a highway. In no mood to hear my excuses, he brought me to the police station, where they took my fingerprints and a mugshot, then threw me in jail.

Sitting in my cell, I felt frightened and violated, but I had the presence of mind to remember what I had seen over and over in American movies: I was entitled to one phone call. So I summoned the courage to demand one, phoning a friend from back home, another student at Madison. He arrived at 4 a.m. to bail me out.

A few hours later, at my arraignment, I pleaded not guilty, and the judge scheduled a hearing for three months later. When that day finally came, the judges were empathic, apologizing for the way I had been treated and asking me to relate to my government that this episode was a mistake and should not have happened. (Years later I thought about contacting the ACLU to file an official complaint, but instead, I made peace with it and let the episode go.)

Madison in the mid-1970s was a vibrant and exciting place to be a student. The campus was teeming with international students—Iranians, Nigerians, Europeans, Asians. Amidst the activist ferment of the mid-1970s, each group freely and openly expressed its political and cultural identity. The Iranian students were particularly outspoken.

I was a skinny young man, and with my dark skin and afro, could have been mistaken for African American. I struggled with my English and with learning to fit into this unfamiliar environment. My lack of confidence and unfamiliarity with American culture caused me to make a number of mistakes that I was too naïve even to recognize.

Soon after I arrived on campus, the department assigned me to an office that I shared with three other graduate students. When I moved in, one of the first things I did was to buy a large poster of Yassir Arafat, the Palestinian Liberation Organization leader, in his iconic kaffiyeh, brandishing a semiautomatic rifle. Without asking anyone else's opinion, I tacked it to the wall above my desk.

I was hardly the only international student in the department. There were many. And I didn't see other displays of nationality or political messages. I don't know what inspired me to put up that poster, and to do so without consulting any of the others who shared the space with me. At the time, Arafat was a known terrorist. It was 1975, three years after PLO terrorists murdered eleven Israeli athletes at the Munich Olympics. Half of the department's faculty and a perhaps a quarter of its students were Jewish, yet it didn't strike me that my choice of décor might offend anyone. It was my attempt to project my identity, no different in my mind from tacking up a flag. I wasn't trying to persuade anyone of anything. Displaying the poster was my way of saying, "This is who I am. This is what I come from. Like it or not, this is what I am about. Deal with it."

If I was looking for confrontation, I was disappointed. Nobody challenged me or even asked me about the poster. Nobody told me to remove it. Nobody tried to argue with me about Mideast politics. The chemical engineering department had more than its share of Jews, both students and professors. Perhaps seeing the poster made them steer clear of me in ways I didn't perceive at the time. But nobody challenged me or even made me feel uncomfortable about the poster.

⌀⌀⌀

ASIDE FROM PLACING THE POSTER ON MY OFFICE WALL, I ENGAGED very little in politics. Most of my friends in Madison were from Libya or other Arab countries. One of my closest friends was Rahuma, an undergraduate in my department who came from Fezzan, the same Libyan region as I did. He was a kind, gentle person who showed me around campus when I first arrived and regularly invited me to his apartment, where I got to know his friends and acquaintances, mostly other Arab students.

In many ways, I was not prepared for American culture, and certainly not for student culture, with all of its freedom and diversity. I lived alone, my English was quite limited, and I was largely on my own, feeling secure (falsely, I would realize later) in my privacy. I was simply more comfortable speaking Arabic and naturally gravitated toward people with similar cultural backgrounds. Many of our conversations centered on the Arab-Israeli conflict. Back in Libya, I hadn't been particularly active politically, but as I tried to sort out my identity in this new culture, my Libyan nationalism was a starting point. I didn't take part in political or cultural organizations on campus, but I defined myself and viewed myself as Libyan, Arab, and Muslim.

My first autumn in Madison, an administrator invited me along with a few other international students for Thanksgiving dinner, the first I had ever experienced. The family happened to be African-American, and they hosted an Iranian student and a Nigerian student along with me. The gathering was considered to be so unusual that a local television station covered it, and I made my debut on American TV.

⎯⎯ ⧉ ⎯⎯

MORE AND MORE, THOUGH, I PRIORITIZED SOMETHING ELSE: having fun. For years back in Tripoli—and before that in Sebha—I had been driven by pressure and ambition, working hard to stay at the top academically and earn my way to a scholarship. Now that I was in America, with all of its new freedom and opportunities, I found myself wanting simply to enjoy myself. That meant indulging in many of the things college students did in the early 1970s: dancing in nightclubs, drinking, smoking marijuana, traveling on weekends, buying clothes, dining in restaurants. One of my favorite activities in the spring and summertime happened outside the Memorial Library, where people would gather and bring their favorite record albums to play. Anyone could bring a vinyl album and a DJ would put it on a turntable for everyone to dance to. Activities of that sort helped me to open up, enjoy myself, and meet people outside of the narrow circles I had initially clung to out of insecurity and lack of confidence.

For the first time in my life, I also started getting to know women. Back in Libya, from the time I was a child, I had been in environments where boys and girls lived mostly separate lives with little interaction. The assumption was that when the time came, my parents would choose a bride for me.

In America, of course, I discovered an entirely different culture, in which girls and women studied, worked, and socialized alongside men as equals. Because I had been separated from women for so much of my life, at first I thought of them only as sexual objects. But as I got to know young women, I learned that they were just as intelligent as men and, of course, had all sorts of interests besides sex.

One weekend during my second year in Wisconsin, I went to visit a Libyan friend who was living in Milwaukee, about eighty miles east of Madison. At a nightclub one night, I struck up a conversation with a pretty, petite blonde woman named Brenda. She was funny and outgoing, and I enjoyed talking to her. We exchanged telephone numbers, and a week later she called and asked if she could come visit me in Madison. She did, and we had a great time. Brenda had a young child from a previous relationship, but that didn't bother me. We enjoyed each other's company, and she became my girlfriend.

TWO NEW EXPERIENCES IN AMERICA WERE TRANSFORMATIVE FOR me: one was getting to know Jewish people for the first time. The other was the opportunity to consider multiple points of view on important subjects rather than simply accepting one narrow approach. Before long, I discovered that Jewish people were all around me: many of the professors in my department—including my closest mentors—were Jewish, as were a significant portion of the department's students. One summer I spent many long afternoons lounging in the Memorial Student Union facing lake Mendota with some friends and a philosophy professor who happened to be Jewish who engaged us in lengthy, open discussions about life, religion, and politics.

I quickly came to a realization: none of the Jewish

people I met matched the stereotypes I had grown up with of Jews as ugly, power-hungry, evil people. In fact, these Jews were quite the opposite. These were lovely, intelligent, generous, and open people. Even without realizing it, I would come into discussions with rigid, black-and-white, nationalistic positions—the mindset with which I had been raised and educated. That didn't stop the Jewish people I knew from interacting with me. They were open to encountering points of view different from theirs. They didn't shy from sharing their opinions, but for the most part, they were open, tolerant, and engaged. Again and again, I encountered Jewish people and found them to be lovely, thoughtful, kind, and reasonable.

I had been raised to despise Jewish people, though I had never met one. Now that I was getting to know them, I didn't have a single negative interaction with a Jewish person. That gave me pause. For the first time, I began to reexamine my life, to reconsider the way I had been raised. My parents, my community, and my educators in Libya had portrayed the world to me in a way that was turning out to be counter to reality. I began to question that black-and-white, good-and-evil worldview.

That realization planted a seed in me. And I began to think in a more open way, to realize that it wasn't a weakness to consider viewpoints besides my own, to take into account other people's life experience. I began to see how rigidly I had perceived the world and my place in it, and now I came to realize that another way of experiencing the world was possible. I wasn't bound to any particular credo. I opened up to the possibility of listening, observing, and coming to my own understanding. Bit by bit, little by little, I began to experience the world in a new way.

The more I examined my life and my attitudes, the more I realized how wrong I had been, how the closed culture of my upbringing had misled me and filled me with prejudice and even hatred. I had never thought of myself as bigoted or narrow-minded, but now I realized that I had been taught to hate whole categories of people without ever meeting them or learning about them. The culture I had come from didn't allow room for debate or questioning or even much discussion. Now that I saw that the world wasn't what I had been taught it was, and that there were other ways to be in the world, I felt myself becoming more open.

Of course, if I were another person, encountering the open society of the United States might have had the opposite effect: I might have been more resistant to this more tolerant culture. Two aspects of my background influenced me to take the approach I did.

One was my maternal grandmother, the person to whom I felt closest as a child. She was the one who told me stories, who nurtured me, and who shared the kind of worldly wisdom I never received from my parents. Her central message was to be open and loving—to be a good listener. That resonated then with me and continues to inform my choices and outlook.

The other factor was my scientific training. As long as I had been engaged in scientific research—from high school in Sebha to university in Tripoli and now in Madison—I had learned the importance of examining things from many different points of view, of always asking questions, and letting one question lead to another. My science mentors had always taught me that I should continually seek more information. My scientific work was a process of constant inquiry. Why, I wondered, should I approach the rest of the world any differently? Why shouldn't I be constantly asking and wondering and seeking evidence rather than simply accepting what someone told me?

The more I inquired on my own, the more I collected my own evidence about people, the more I came to realize that everything I had been told about Jews was wrong. Everything. I didn't have a single negative experience with a Jewish person. That realization prompted me to begin examining every aspect of my life and belief—religious, political, cultural, social. I wanted to rely on my own evidence, not the lies I had been told.

That process of reexamination also led me to another realization: I wanted to marry a Jewish woman. I didn't have a particular Jewish woman in mind. However, my new introspection had inspired me to leave behind the doctrinaire, narrow set of beliefs I had inherited. This enlightenment started with a germ of an idea—that I wanted to get closer to Jewish people, to be more intimate. And that grew to a desire to marry a Jewish woman. Perhaps it would be a way to cleanse myself of the hateful mindset that had infiltrated my thinking for so many years.

———————⌘———————

I RETURNED HOME TO LIBYA ONLY TWICE DURING MY YEARS AT Wisconsin. In 1978, I received notice in the midst of the school year that Gaddafi had issued a request that every Libyan student studying in the United States return to the country for a mandatory meeting. The timing of the meeting was particularly inconvenient for me: it conflicted with some of my final exams. But the government offered me no alternative. Since Libya was financing my education and covering all of my expenses, not honoring the invitation might have jeopardized my scholarship—and my future.

So, I flew to Tripoli, where the government hosted our large student delegation at a camp facility near Gaddafi's compound. During the week we stayed there, the government pampered us, catering delicious meals, offering tours of ancient Greek and Roman ruins by day and entertaining us with movies and live theater by night. It felt like a vacation, without any particular agenda. We didn't meet with Col. Gaddafi himself, but his representatives communicated a strong nationalist agenda and a clear message to each of us: Libya is paying for your education, and you are beholden to us; we expect you to support Col. Gaddafi openly, and we look forward to your returning to Libya when you finish your academic work so that you can support the regime and help us to build the country.

It didn't take much imagination to understand that Gaddafi and his people had a darker purpose in summoning us all to Libya. At that point, Gaddafi had begun his practice of rounding up anyone he perceived as an enemy and disposing of those people. It was his way of solidifying his control of the country. Among the group of students, Gaddafi's people had singled out a few students who had become outspoken in their opposition to Gaddafi. During our week there, some of them quietly disappeared. I assumed they had been sent to prison. (Gaddafi's regime had a notorious prison called Abu Salim.)

While I was vaguely aware of what was transpiring, I didn't worry about my own safety or well-being. Since I had never been politically active or outspoken—in Tripoli or in Madison—I didn't fear that harm would come to me. But perceiving what was happening, I concluded that I wanted

no part of this regime. I wanted to get as far as I could from
Gaddafi and from Libya, and I wanted to stay away. The
best way to do that was to stay out of trouble, to focus on
my work, and not to call attention to myself.

EVEN BEFORE THE TRIP BACK TO TRIPOLI, I HAD BEEN QUESTION-
ing my upbringing and everything that came with the nationalistic mindset of my upbringing. Returning to Madison, I
felt even more strongly that my future was in America. At
the same time that I was considering the conflict between
my home country and my adopted home, I also began to
question whether I was on the right course academically.
Wisconsin's chemical engineering department wasn't rated
number one without good reason. It was intensely demanding, and for a student to succeed academically meant sacri-
ficing just about everything else. I began to question whether
achieving at that level was truly a higher priority than some
of the other things that had become important to me: social
life, friends, having fun. In short, I became less focused on
academic achievement and more on being aware of how I
could contribute to our world.

The students who excelled in Wisconsin's program
approached their academics with great seriousness and an
exceedingly strong work ethic, leaving no time for anything
else. They took the highest-level courses, attached themselves to faculty mentors, and engaged in serious scientific
research. The reward at the end was that most graduates of
the department landed plum positions at top universities.
But my mind simply wasn't there. I was a good student,
but I also wanted time to find myself—and to play. I knew I

wanted to finish my doctoral degree, but not at the expense of having a full, rich, and textured life.

I began to investigate the possibility transferring to another university. I had friends in Los Angeles who spoke fondly of living there, so I applied to UCLA, USC, and Caltech. I was accepted at USC and decided to enroll. I notified the Libyan government that I was transferring, and they agreed to continue funding my education. If it meant I would complete my degree and return to serve Libya, they were supportive. In the fall of 1978, with great excitement I left Madison for sunny Los Angeles.

CHAPTER 6

Freedom, Possibility, and Love in California

———— ᘐᘐᘐ ————

Nothing prepared me for the metropolis of Los Angeles, but a friend helped to ease my landing. Ahmed Shawky was a classmate from my years in the chemical engineering department at the University of Tripoli. Now he was working in Libya for an oil company, Occidental Petroleum Corporation, which had sent him to study at the University of California at Irvine. Occidental's owner, Armand Hammer, was a friend of Libya's King Idris and discovered oil in Libya in the 1960s, transforming it from a very poor country to a very rich one. Ahmed flew to Madison and together we drove west in my new blue Camero. We were on the road for about a week, stopping in Boise, Idaho, where his sister was living with her husband, a student at the University of Idaho. When we arrived in Southern California, Ahmed invited me to stay with him at a furnished apartment he had rented in Newport Beach until I had a place of my own.

Los Angeles's weather reminded me of Tripoli's Mediterranean climate, but the city was so sprawling that it was difficult for a newcomer to learn to navigate. Newport Beach, on the other hand, was picturesque and pleasant, and I was happy being near the ocean. I briefly considered selling the Camero to buy a boat, but reality got in the way. I commuted for a time to USC from Newport Beach, but after just a few months, the commute through traffic became too much of a burden.

Wanting to be closer to campus, I moved to an apartment in Hollywood, near Vermont Avenue and Sunset Boulevard. The commute to campus was easier, but I found it difficult to adjust to the neighborhood, which I found unpleasant—dirty, noisy, and crowded with all kinds of people.

Despite that, I felt almost immediately that the transfer to USC was the right move. I passed the qualifying exam for the chemical engineering department, and promptly started on my research. I chose to study the complexity of carbon monoxide oxidation over platinum as a catalyst (a field that had applications in the automobile industry) and chemical reaction engineering in general. I set up my own laboratory. It was the first time I had ever worked with my hands to set up equipment and designed vessels. Carbon monoxide is highly toxic, so we had to be extremely careful in handling it. I was proud of my work establishing the laboratory and establishing a new organization for engineering graduate students, chartered by USC's School of Engineering and modeled after similar groups at other universities.

I also began developing friendships with graduate students in other departments. Every Friday the university held "TGIF" socials to give students the opportunity to connect. Back in Madison, I had mostly socialized with other Arab students, but at USC I took advantage of the diverse student population, forging friendships with students from Korea, China, and many other countries. I went to some football games but otherwise didn't get particularly involved in campus life.

———∘∞∘———

ONE THING I DID FOR FUN AND EXERCISE WAS PLAY TENNIS. I
had never been particularly athletic. After my struggles
with serious illness during middle school, sports didn't feel
like an option. In Wisconsin, I had bought a basketball and
played a bit, but the one sport I pursued was tennis, which
I occasionally played with Brenda, my Wisconsin girlfriend,
and others. When I moved to Los Angeles, I asked around
about local tennis facilities. Someone suggested the athletic
club at the Ambassador Hotel near downtown, where the
practice featured machines that automatically lobbed tennis
balls. I started playing there a few times a week, paying a
dollar or so each time for thirty minutes to practice my swing.

One early evening in late June of 1979, I was alone on
the practice court at the Ambassador Hotel when I realized
there was a someone just outside the hitting cage, a lovely
lady in her mid-twenties waiting for me to finish so she could
take her turn. She reminded me that my time was up, and I
started picking up the balls I had used to clear the court for
her. She joined in. As I was stepping off the court, I asked,
"Do you mind if I sit outside and watch you?"

I will never know why I made that request. She said she
didn't mind, and for a few minutes, I sat, not saying anything, and watching her practice her swing. After a while,
I walked back to the clubhouse. As I was getting ready to
leave, I noticed someone approaching me. It was the same
woman. She smiled.

"Hi, my name's Barbara," she said. "What's your name?
"Abdulhafied," I said.
She asked where I was from.
"Libya," I told her. "I go to USC."

She asked if I'd like to hit some balls together. "Sure," I said. Barbara inquired at the clubhouse and lined up a court for us.

As we walked together toward the court, she said, "By the way, I just want you to know, I'm Jewish." I wasn't sure why she felt the need to tell me, but I appreciated her openness. Of course, that didn't bother me. We spent a half hour or so volleying on a court. I enjoyed it. Before we parted, we exchanged telephone numbers.

As I left the Ambassador Hotel, I contemplated what had happened: I had told myself I wanted to marry a Jewish woman. And here, one had walked into my life.

I wanted to see her again, but I didn't call her. Perhaps I was questioning my own judgment: was this really what I wanted? Was I ready for this? A week later, Barbara called. We got together and played tennis again at the Ambassador Hotel, where it turned out her parents had a membership at the athletic club.

Afterward, I asked if she wanted to get a bite. We stopped for drinks and hors d'oeuvres on the outdoor patio of El Cholo, a Mexican restaurant on Western Avenue.

I immediately liked Barbara. We both enjoyed tennis. I was accustomed to women playing hard-to-get or somehow hiding their desires or intentions. She was different. Barbara had a forthright, matter-of-fact manner that I found refreshing.

As it happened, I was planning to leave two days later for a week in Puerto Vallarta. I had been working hard to prepare for the entrance exam for the doctoral degree program and needed a break from the workload. When I returned to Los Angeles, I discovered a note Barbara had left on my apartment door, saying that she missed me and wanted to get together again soon. It made me happy to know she was thinking about me.

I PHONED BARBARA AND ASKED HER OUT TO A STEAKHOUSE IN Studio City. She asked me to pick her up at the home she shared with her parents, the upstairs unit of a duplex they owned on Detroit Street, in the Fairfax area. When I arrived, the whole family was there eating dinner: her father and mother and her younger sister and the sister's boyfriend. Barbara had already told me that her father, Robert Levin, who was born in Pinsk, Poland, had emigrated to Palestine and fought in Israel's War of Independence. He also could speak or read ten different languages. Her sister's boyfriend, Mooky, was an Israeli who had fought in the Israel Defense Forces. Barbara's mother, Ellen, grew up in Stamford, Connecticut, the grandchild of Jewish immigrants from Russia.

She told me later the entire family thought she had lost her mind when she told them she was dating a man from Libya. But the truth was that we got along well. Barbara's father had strong opinions about the Arab-Israeli conflict, but he approached me not as an "Arab," but an individual. We enjoyed discussing the commonalities of Hebrew and Arabic. On a deeper level, we were both survivors of sorts, each of us born into one culture and eventually finding our way to another.

As for Barbara, she had a strong Jewish identity, but not much of a Jewish education. She had spent time in Israel in 1973, volunteering at a kibbutz called Beit Alfa, in the Galilee, during the Yom Kippur War. As an adult, she had become more of a spiritual explorer, open to various traditions and experiences.

We had gone on only a few dates when Barbara told me she was considering moving into an apartment her parents owned in Koreatown, at Ninth Street and Vermont Avenue. It was convenient to her work at Kaiser Sunset, where she worked as a medical stenographer. She didn't feel entirely comfortable living in the neighborhood on her own, so she asked if I'd liked to move in with her.

I didn't immediately seize the opportunity. The location would make for an easy commute to USC's campus, but I wasn't sure I was ready. I told her that I enjoyed our friendship, but I wasn't really ready to make a commitment.

"No commitment," she told me. "It's just two friends, sharing the rent. You can do whatever you want with your life."

After I gave it some thought, I called Barbara and we arranged to meet to discuss the idea. We met for dinner at the Bob's Big Boy on Wilshire Boulevard near Highland. I set the ground rules: I don't want you to have high expectations. This isn't necessarily a love relationship. We'll be roommates. Barbara agreed, and in August of 1979, we moved in together.

At first, sharing the apartment was mostly a matter of mutual convenience and safety. We enjoyed each other's company, but we weren't planning a life together. I gave Barbara her space, and she gave me mine. She frequently socialized with friends. I had only a few close friends at USC with whom I socialized occasionally, but mostly I focused on my academic work.

Barbara also helped me to grow in unexpected ways. She is a talented artist, and I admired her drawing, particularly since I could barely draw a stick figure myself. But Barbara encouraged me, buying me the book *Drawing on the Right Side of the Brain* by Betty Edwards, which I studied intently. I spent several weeks following its exercises, sometimes losing myself for hours in the process of pencil drawing. Not only did drawing give me a creative outlet, but it provided a relaxing and meditative diversion from my busy academic life.

OVER TIME, WHAT HAD BEGUN AS A ROOMMATE SITUATION BEGAN transforming into something more serious. Barbara helped me with my schoolwork, even showing up occasionally at the USC campus to bring me lunch. And we became closer in other ways, sharing our lives and stories and helping each other through our daily challenges.

Always direct, Barbara didn't hesitate to share that she wanted us to be closer, even professing her love. As much as I enjoyed her company, something in me resisted. For so long I had been on my own, a survivor, relying on no one but myself. I also had a fear of commitment. I didn't know where my academic work would lead and I didn't want limitations.

That was in my head. But then I started listening to my heart, and, in time, I realized I felt love—deep love—for Barbara. For the first time since early childhood, I had someone I truly wanted to share my life with. We came from starkly different backgrounds, but in many ways, we were kindred spirits, both searching for direction, for meaning, and for connection.

As our love bond grew deeper and stronger, I learned that Barbara had always been independent and strong-minded. She wasn't a rebel, exactly—in fact, she was always close to her parents. But after high school, she had once moved out of the house and moved with a boyfriend to Arizona. She was certainly ready to move out of her parent's home.

Was moving in with me a form of rebellion? It was true

that her father was a typical Israeli: tough, strongminded, and certainly not trusting of Arabs. But the family wasn't particularly religious. Their only regular Jewish observance consisted of an annual Passover Seder and exchanging gifts for Hanukkah.

The first time the family invited me to a Passover Seder, I was thoroughly confused. The Haggadah they used was a simple version that had been assembled by an elementary-school teacher. The family paid only limited attention to the text or the messages of Passover. What made more of an impression on me was the food: matzah-ball soup, gefilte fish, brisket. It was delicious and plentiful.

LACKING MUCH IN THE WAY OF RELIGIOUS UPBRINGING, BARBARA was in the midst of a sort of search for a meaningful spiritual life. She had a close friend, Clark, who was an Ob-Gyn at UCLA in his forties and was an active Christian. He was a quasi-father figure to Barbara, occasionally bringing her along to experience various churches. One of them was Pastor Rick Warren's Saddleback Church in Orange County, which was then relatively new.

Though I wasn't actively seeking spirituality or religion, I, too, sometimes felt a spiritual vacuum. The version of Islam I had grown up with had never spoken to me. I hadn't ever gone to a mosque in Madison or Los Angeles—though I certainly knew many people who were practicing Muslims. I socialized with other Arab and Muslim students, and I knew there was a large mosque near USC's campus, but I had long since moved away from Islam, and didn't consider it part of my life.

Still, some of my early explorations along with Barbara proved to be interesting, but not exactly fulfilling. On at least one occasion, I accompanied Barbara and Clark to Saddleback Church. I found it to be a fascinating spectacle, with lots of music and evangelizing, full of chants of "Praise the Lord!" and testimonials about the power of accepting Jesus. I was fascinated and saw how it could be appealing to many people, but it didn't speak to my needs or desires.

What I found more appealing was a church called the Hollywood Church of Religious Science, on Sunset Boulevard in Hollywood. Barbara and I started attending on Sunday mornings together. There, a tiny, elderly minister named Dr. Robert Bitzer gave sermons full of compassion and that appealed to reason. He talked about how to be good to yourself and to your neighbor. And Bitzer himself came across as sweet and kind.

Being in Hollywood, the church had its share of celebrity congregants, and the organist was a lively performer named Stan Kann, who was famous for his animated appearances on "The Tonight Show" and "The Merv Griffin Show." What attracted me, though, wasn't the showmanship or the names, but the combination of spirituality and rational thinking. The church was helping people to contemplate big issues: What is God? What is God's purpose? Are our destinies predetermined? Those conversations touched me and made me think. Both Barbara and I had an affinity for the rational approach combined with Bitzer's deep humanity and intelligence. We also learned a great deal from Emmet Fox's books on spirituality and morality.

In 1979, I made what would be my last brief trip back to Libya. My father had now married a second wife, Masuda, who had previously been married to his late brother, and with whom he had a son and daughter. He welcomed me with pride, and relatives and neighbors filled the house day and night as my father and stepmother offered delicious meals and tea to anyone who visited. Everyone had the same question: When would I be moving back home? I listened and smiled, but inside, I knew the answer: I wouldn't be returning. After discovering a new life, with its openness, opportunities, and possibility, I could not imagine coming back to Libya, to that way of life, or to that oppressive culture. I felt a distance from the place of my birth, but also gratitude that I was forging a path of my own choosing.

Before I left Hatiet Bergen for the last time, I presented my father with a gift: the money I had accumulated in Libya from my year as a college teacher. It was probably five times my father's annual salary. Though our relationship had long been strained, I felt gratified to see his pride in my accomplishments and a sense of satisfaction that I was able to offer him some degree of financial support.

Back in Los Angeles, my relationship with Barbara grew over time into something more significant. In many ways, I felt alone in the world. My grandmother, who nurtured me as a child, had been gone for years. My mother had died when I was in college. My brother and father were still in Libya, but we were rarely in touch.

With Barbara, though, I enjoyed a human connection that had eluded me for much of my life. We came from different

worlds, but she cared for me. She took interest in my academic work and every detail of my life. She made me feel
loved and appreciated. For the first time since childhood, I
felt a sense of belonging and caring, and she brought me
great happiness.

I realized I wanted to marry her. I figured I should get her
a ring. A relative of Barbara's family owned a jewelry store
in downtown Los Angeles, so I got the measurements for
Barbara's ring finger and in December of 1980 purchased a
ring. Barbara and I were planning a getaway to Palm Springs
and knew we would be playing tennis, as we often did. I took
a can of tennis balls, removed the middle of the three balls,
and replaced it with the box holding the ring. That weekend,
we were on the tennis courts when I handed her the can of
balls and asked her to open it. Inside, she discovered the
box, opening it to reveal the ring. She flashed a surprised
and delighted smile.

"Will you marry me?" I asked.

"I will," she said.

We planned a wedding for just two weeks later, on
December 26, 1980, at Barbara's parents' house on North
Detroit Street. Barbara's grandparents and her Aunt Betty
were to be visiting from Connecticut; her grandparents
often visited for a couple of weeks in the winter to enjoy the
warmer weather.

A month or so before the ceremony, Barbara and I attended
the wedding of one of her colleagues. We were impressed
with the minister, a nondenominational minister who was
open to performing intermarriages. We asked him to officiate
at our wedding, and he agreed.

Barbara and I worked together to create our own ceremony, partly based on teachings from Science of Mind.

Together, we wrote vows that emphasized our commitment to each other and to the significance of joining our two cultures and living ethically. We felt that if an Arab and a Jew could create a family together, there was hope for the world, and we wanted to share that hope and make it an inspiration. (See page 172 to read the wedding vows we wrote and recited.)

We had about three dozen guests, all from Barbara's side: besides her grandparents and aunt, there were her sisters, cousins, and many close family friends. Despite the differences in our backgrounds, Barbara's parents were very accepting of me and supportive of us as a couple, and their family followed their lead.

My family, on the other hand, didn't even know I was getting married. I had not told my father about my relationship with Barbara—not because I was ashamed, but because our life was so far from his life experience that I didn't think he could possibly understand. In fact, I had shared the information with almost none of my handful of Libyan friends in the United States. I had one Libyan friend who was a year behind me in the department at USC, but I didn't tell him about the wedding. I invited only one friend, Rahuma, whom I had met at Wisconsin and who was then at Ohio State University, but he wasn't able to make it.

I suppose I also felt some sense of insecurity. Nearly all of my friends were students, and many of them were Muslims. I feared that might make for an awkward mix.

My lack of guests at the wedding was reflective of how I saw myself. I was a survivor. I had managed to persevere in the jungle of life. I had overcome obstacles and found my own way to accomplish and achieve on my own terms. But I had done that in large part by isolating myself. Besides

Barbara, I didn't have close friends. I wasn't a particularly open person. I kept a lot inside. Perhaps that was simply the model I had learned since childhood from watching my father and other men in my life. Back in the village, women had wailed publicly after experiencing deaths in their families and openly shouted with glee at happy occasions, but the men kept things inside. That model of how men coped with their feelings had a strong influence on how I processed emotions—or failed to. I did little reflection or introspection. Sometimes I couldn't sort out whether I felt sad, perplexed, angry, or annoyed. I wasn't comfortable in my own skin, and I rarely shared my feelings.

In any case, I was on my own. On the morning of our wedding day, Barbara left our apartment and headed to her parents' house, leaving me at home. That afternoon, I put on the white tuxedo I had rented and drove to the house. There, some guests, noticing how nervous I was, offered me a glass of champagne. Barbara's grandparents, Morris and Eve Folb, served as the witnesses for our marriage certificate.

The ceremony was a blur. Barbara's younger sister, Julie, sang and a woman played piano. At the end, I stepped on a glass—one of our few nods to the Jewish tradition—the music picked up, and then everyone feasted.

Barbara and I left the next day for a honeymoon road trip to San Francisco, stopping along the way at Santa Barbara, San Simeon, and Big Sur.

As it turned out, Barbara helped me through a very difficult time in my academic and professional life. I was working on my dissertation, but I had a rocky relationship with Theodore, the professor who was overseeing my work.

USC's chemical engineering department was relatively small, with only a handful of professors, and Theodore was the only one who specialized in kinetics and chemical-reactions engineering, a hot field and the topic I had chosen to pursue. He was only slightly more experienced than I was, having earned his doctorate only a year before I became the first doctoral student he was assigned to supervise.

At first, that arrangement had its advantages. Since there were so few doctoral students and little research going on in the chemical engineering department at the time, Theodore and I worked almost as peers, collaborating on outlining the scope of my thesis and in submitting theoretical work for publication. We worked together to set up a first-class laboratory from scratch, starting from an empty room.

But over time, I became resistant to Theodore's authority. His own thesis had been theoretical, so he had little hands-on lab experience, so I found it difficult to see him as an expert from whom I could learn. The arrangement brought out the worst in me: the more we worked together, the worse my attitude about the collaboration.

When I was nearing the end of my doctoral work, I came to realize another problem: Theodore would not be of much assistance to me in securing a position either in academia or in industry, because he simply lacked the kind of network that would have been helpful. I had erred in not developing more relationships in the field, connections that would have helped me find work down the line.

In the spring of 1982, I finally let Theodore know that I was finished with my doctoral work, and I asked him to sign off on my dissertation. He did not react well.

"You don't tell me what to do," Theodore said. "I'm the professor."

That touched off a confrontation. I told him that while it was true that he was the professor, since I was his first student, it would be beneficial to his reputation if I went on to success.

I won that battle in the short-term, but in the longer term, I suffered; as I moved on from USC, I found myself on my own, without much support. I would need a strong recommendation from my advisor to secure work, whether in industry or academia, and I was worried that after our conflict, Theodore simply wouldn't be able to deliver.

It was Barbara who helped me through that difficult and challenging period. She worked tirelessly to help type my dissertation. And then, as I launched my job search, she helped me compile my résumé and send out job applications by the hundreds. I applied to practically any position that looked possible: research and development positions at oil companies and automobile manufacturers, academic jobs, opportunities with environmental organizations.

One possibility I was very excited about was a two-year research fellowship at the Jet Propulsion Laboratory in Pasadena. I put a great deal of work into a proposal for an innovative research project and submitted it to JPL. I came very close to winning the fellowship, but then security became an issue. I was still a Libyan citizen, in the process of applying for U.S. citizenship. Relations between the two countries were so strained that I wasn't able to get security clearance. That unfortunate reality ended my hopes of working at JPL.

When I was in the midst of the application process, a few friends and members of Barbara's family suggested that my name might be an obstacle in the job hunt. Perhaps seeing the name Abdulhafied at the top of my CV might be off-putting to hiring managers, creating a stigma. They suggested that a more American-sounding name might be helpful.

I was open to that idea. My full name was Abdulhafied Elsaidi Elhaderi. I wanted to preserve my initials, but decided to adopt a name that started with "E," corresponding with my middle name. I considered a few: Edwin, Ernest, Elliott. I decided I liked Edward: A. Edward Elhaderi. I wasn't a citizen yet, but I simply started using the name and wrote a letter to my USC professors letting them know that I was now Edward, and to make them aware that they might receive correspondence from potential employers inquiring about an A. Edward Elhaderi.

As it turned out, the new name didn't make much difference in my job hunt. In all, I sent out—with Barbara's help—more than five hundred job applications. I secured only about five job interviews. None of those turned into jobs, and after a couple of months searching, I found myself at a dead-end.

For the first time in my life, I was facing abject failure, and it was difficult to determine why. For much of my life—since I went off to middle school in Sebha—I had felt on my own in the world. I had managed to survive on my instincts, making my way in this new country. My natural inclination wasn't to reach out to others for help but rather to be as independent and self-reliant as possible. I had successfully achieved much of what I set my mind to. But now I was learning the limitations of that approach: perhaps my impulse to do my own thing had prevented me from forging the kinds of connections at USC that would have helped me in securing employment.

Not only had I not cultivated relationships with mentors

who might have helped guide me through this process, but I also hadn't forged close friendships with other students. I had acquaintances at the university, but I couldn't consider any of them close friends, the kinds of people with whom I could commiserate or unload my troubles.

In short, I had a beautiful marriage, but I lacked a community.

⁓⊗⊗⊗⁓

AROUND THE TIME WE MARRIED, I HAD APPLIED FOR AMERICAN citizenship. The Immigration and Naturalization Service requires a five-year wait before it will approve an application. In August of 1985, I had an appointment at the Federal Building in downtown Los Angeles for an interview. The immigration agent asked me some questions about myself and quizzed me about some basics facts about the United States. I passed and earned my U.S. citizenship. Then came an unexpected question. As the clerk was filling out the paperwork, he asked, "Would you like to take the opportunity to change your name?" He explained that it was a chance to do so without incurring any additional cost or hassle.

I had already been using the name Edward for nearly five years. I wanted to maintain the initials A.E. (for Abdulhafied Elsaid) Elhaderi. I assumed it would be simply A. Edward Elhaderi. But when the clerk inquired, I asked for a minute to consult with Barbara.

Barbara suggested that I change my last name to Hartley. Elhaderi had strong "H" sound, so it would be honoring that, but had a more American sound. (Mariette Hartley was a popular TV actress at the time.) "A. Edward Hartley." I liked the sound of it: distinguished, simple, easy to say—and American.

Barbara and I agreed and I returned to the clerk with the new name. We completed the paperwork, and together, Barbara and I walked out of the building and onto the street.

Almost immediately, I felt a sense of regret—an almost physical sense of nausea and disgust. I felt as if my world was collapsing around me. What had I done? I felt like I had allowed myself to be robbed of my existence. I had cut off my connection to my heritage and ancestors. I didn't recognize myself. What had I been thinking in changing my last name on a whim?

I stopped walking. "I feel terrible," I told Barbara. "I don't want my name to be Hartley. My name is Elhaderi."

I didn't have to explain further. Together, we returned to the citizenship office and found the official who had helped with my paperwork.

"I made a mistake," I said. "I want to keep my name, Elhaderi. I don't want to change it."

"It's too late," he said. "You signed and the paperwork went through." Only a few minutes had passed, but he assured me that undoing my decision wouldn't be simple. My only option was to go through a court process to change my name back. For now, I was Edward Hartley.

I never used that name, except on the INS form that day. I continued to use the last name Elhaderi, and never told anyone about my new name. Soon after, I hired a lawyer to help me through the process of regaining my original surname. The process took several months. Finally, the following November, the court approved my name change from A. Edward Hartley, back to A. Edward Elhaderi. To me, it was worth the cost and the aggravation to have my name—and my identity—back intact. I was delighted to go forward in life as A. Edward Elhaderi—officially.

DESPITE MY DIFFICULTY FINDING WORK, I HAD CLEARLY RULED
out one path: I wouldn't be returning to Libya. Now that I
was married to Barbara, I wouldn't even consider it. Financially, it certainly would have made sense. I would have had
a teaching position or, probably, my choice of high-level jobs
in Libya's government or petroleum industry.

But I no longer felt any emotional pull, no cord of connection. Perhaps things would have been different if my
mother hadn't died, but my relationship with my father
wasn't close. At best, it was neutral. After my last visit, in
1979, I had only minimal contact. When we spoke, he had
only two questions: "How are you doing?" and "When are
you coming back?"

At one point, I sat down and wrote my father a long letter.
I never intended to send it to him, but it helped me sort out
my complicated feelings about my relationship with him
that had been weighing on me. I felt I couldn't move forward
without taking some time to reflect, and Barbara strongly
supported the idea as a form of therapy for myself.

In the letter, I asked my father for forgiveness for any
harm I had caused him and for failing to meet his expectations in any way. In Libyan culture, the eldest male is
expected to care for his mother and father in their later years.
In fact, one of the primary reasons to have children at all is
to insure that you have someone to till the land and handle
physical labor of the farm and household, and to look after
your well-being when you can no longer do so on your own.

Certainly, my father had my younger brother to help
him, as well as other relatives. But when he asked when I
was coming back, the implication was that I was shirking

my responsibility. I apologized for disappointing him, and I also forgave him for any harm he had done to me.

The letter was three or four pages. When I finished it, I folded it, sealed it in an envelope, and placed it in the back of a drawer. I never sent it.

The only other relative I maintained any contact with was my brother, Abdullatif, who eventually became an educator and then the principal at a technical school in Sebha. During my childhood, he always looked up to me, though we spent little time in the same place except during my middle-school years in Sebha. After I moved to Los Angeles, he called occasionally, and always had the same question as my father: When are you coming back? We are waiting for you.

The answer, of course, was: never.

Before I had left for the University Wisconsin, I had signed documents pledging to return to Libya once I finished my education. In a sense, I felt a moral obligation to keep my word. On the other hand, at the time, Muammar Gaddafi had emerged as a brutal terrorist tyrant, targeting his opponents in Europe, Asia, and elsewhere, and I had very real fears that one day his agents would abduct me in the streets of Los Angeles and transport me back to Libya. I was haunted by the scene in the 1985 movie Back to the Future in which Libyan terrorists suddenly appear in a van, shooting at Christopher Lloyd's character. For years I suffered from nightmares: I would be walking on the USC campus or near home and thugs with guns appeared and grabbed me. (Occasionally I also had more pleasant dreams about being home with my family or in Tripoli.)

The reality was that I probably didn't have reason to worry. I had never been politically active or outspoken, in Libya or in the United States, so I didn't call attention to myself. And I had many friends and acquaintances from high school and university who had risen to prominent positions in the Gaddafi government. I knew they wouldn't do me harm—or at least I had convinced myself that they wouldn't.

The one contact I received more or less confirmed my suspicion. Uloa, a classmate I had been friendly with in high school back in Sebha, phoned at one point to encourage me to return to Libya. He had gone on to university in Greece and returned to assume a prominent position in the Libyan navy.

"Your country needs you," he told me. "You have a good name here. You are admired." He assured me that I would have my choice of positions and could create my own destiny in Libya. I told him I would think about what he said, but the truth was that I had made up my mind long before. I wouldn't be going back.

That didn't mean I could escape my identity as a Libyan—nor did I want to. By the mid-1980s, Libya had become a pariah state. In April of 1986, after terrorists bombed a Berlin discotheque frequented by U.S. soldiers, President Reagan blamed Libya, and the U.S. military carried out air bombing strikes of Tripoli and Benghazi. Shortly after that, I went with a group of friends to the Comedy Store on Sunset Boulevard. One of the comedians mentioned Gaddafi, and asked, "Are there any Libyans in the audience?" To his obvious surprise, I proudly raised my hand.

I never shied away from revealing my identity or my roots. I had been a Muslim. I was from Libya. I could not deny it. If another person felt uncomfortable with that, it was their problem, not mine. I hadn't done anything wrong and carried no ill will toward anyone.

My struggles to find work presented a personal crisis. Ever since I had entered university at age eighteen, I had been preparing for a career in chemical engineering. If I couldn't work in my field, what would I do? I ruminated, I questioned, and I second-guessed myself. I felt demoralized, even ashamed. It was difficult to accept that after all those years of effort, I had failed to find work in my chosen field.

As I struggled with the direction of my professional life, I found guidance from an unexpected source, the radio. I started listening to a program on Pacifica Radio hosted by Alan Watts, who was a pioneer in bringing Eastern philosophy to popular audiences in the West. He frequently said that if you want to see what's inside your mind, just look in front of you: the way the world looks to you reflects what's going on internally. If you find everything around you to be disgusting and horrible, that's probably the state of your own mind. Being in the present, on the other hand, means having your mind and body in sync, paying attention to this moment. Time stops. You only think about the present—not yesterday, not tomorrow. That eliminates mental anguish.

So instead of simply feeling disappointed, I tried to make peace with my situation. I also had practical considerations: I had to make a living.

I also started reading memoirs and biographies of successful people: Dale Carnegie's *How to Win Friends and Influence People*. Napoleon Hill's *Think and Grow Rich*. Almost every day I went to the library, and I found more and more sources of wisdom.

Another book I came across was *How You Can Become Financially Independent by Investing in Real Estate*. It was by

Albert Lowry, who had managed to accumulate a fortune and now was marketing books and seminars to help others to find their own success. I read *Nothing Down*, Robert Allen's book about how to make money in real estate even if you didn't have any to start with, and then paid four hundred dollars to attend a talk Allen led that attracted a sellout crowd to a large ballroom at Wilshire Boulevard hotel. The country was just beginning to recover from a real-estate recession, so at the time there was great opportunity to invest in properties in need of fixing up. Barbara's parents owned some investment properties, and I was intrigued by the possibility of making a living through real estate.

I decided to make a concerted effort to break into the field. I started by enrolling in a course sponsored by Century 21 Real Estate, in which I learned the basics of real estate and prepared to take the exam for the real-estate license. It was a comprehensive course, covering the many aspects of the field: appraisal, financing, purchasing, sales, and much more.

In December of 1982, I earned my real estate license, and the next month I landed at job at Jon Douglas Co. in West Los Angeles. It was run by Jerry Smith, an enlightened and compassionate mentor who oversaw a team of forty or fifty. It was a diverse, international group, including immigrants from Greece, India, Canada—and, of course, Libya. It was a mutually supportive group, and while I earned a living, what I treasured was the camaraderie and friendships I developed.

A few years later, Barbara and I began looking for a property of our own. Looking in the *Los Angeles Times* classified ads—among the only options at the time—I discovered a lovely four-unit building on Shenandoah Street, less than a block from Beverly Hills.

In 1986, Barbara and I bought the building. It wasn't a neighborhood we had considered (I had never even spent time nearby except for a dental appointment not long after I arrived in Los Angeles), but it was located on a lovely tree-lined street less than half a block from Beverly Hills. We moved in, relocating from the Koreatown apartment where we had been living since we first moved in together, and rented out the other three units to tenants.

I also made that area, known as Pico-Robertson, the focus of my residential real-estate business.

The more experiences I had in real estate, the more I enjoyed it. I was naturally an introvert, so I had to push myself. I was on stage every day, whether I felt like it or not. When you're a salesperson, you cannot hide. I had to knock on doors. I had to send out mailers. I was forced to develop the social aspect of myself. I had to find ways to connect with potential sellers and buyers. Without connections, I wouldn't have had contracts or transactions—or income. But on a good day, I would finish my workday with a sense of accomplishment: I had connected with someone; I had helped a young family purchase their first home; I had helped someone secure financing for their house. It wasn't just about the paperwork or the transactions. I was making a difference in people's lives. Anyone could walk into my office and I had the opportunity to connect with that person and help that person. It was a wonderful feeling.

Being a realtor gave me the opportunity to witness the true diversity and uniqueness of our beautiful country. I have worked with everyone from young people struggling to start their lives to families and businesses with deep connections and great wealth. I have also seen the many aspects of human behavior (the good, the bad, and the ugly), watching the challenges people can face in maintaining relationships during stressful financial transactions. Early on, I was not skillful in fully leveraging my contacts—socially or financially. But the lessons I have learned along the way have been invaluable and they have shaped my views on living an ethical, moral, and compassionate life.

CHAPTER 7

Finding My Inner Self

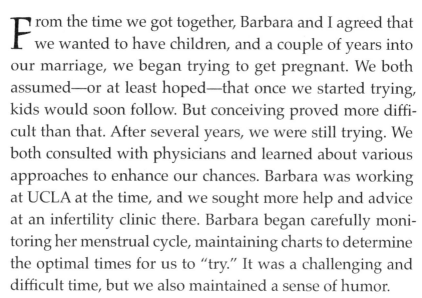

From the time we got together, Barbara and I agreed that we wanted to have children, and a couple of years into our marriage, we began trying to get pregnant. We both assumed—or at least hoped—that once we started trying, kids would soon follow. But conceiving proved more difficult than that. After several years, we were still trying. We both consulted with physicians and learned about various approaches to enhance our chances. Barbara was working at UCLA at the time, and we sought more help and advice at an infertility clinic there. Barbara began carefully monitoring her menstrual cycle, maintaining charts to determine the optimal times for us to "try." It was a challenging and difficult time, but we also maintained a sense of humor.

"Come on, Ed," she would say, "you have to be ready in half an hour!" If I wasn't quite ready, she would urge me on so we could take advantage of the moment. As enjoyable as that sometimes could be, when we still didn't find success, the situation became emotionally challenging for both of us.

The human mind has its ways of coping with these kinds of setbacks. Barbara's reaction was fatalistic: after many months of attempts, she concluded that perhaps we simply weren't meant to have children together. I tried to use reason to think it through, figuring that following professionals' advice would eventually help.

In any case, we both maintained a strong desire to start a family, so we began to explore the option of adopting. One of our first steps was to attend a meeting of an organization called Triad, where we learned about some of the emotional and psychological challenges surrounding adoption. We learned how the process affects adoptive parents and the many issues that can last a lifetime. Often children who are adopted at some point begin asking questions as they try to make sense of their lives. That can take its toll on the child and adoptive parents alike. Clearly, these weren't simply short-term matters, but issues that might emerge at any moment down the line. Triad helped us to face these difficulties openly and directly, and Barbara and I discussed whether we were prepared to take on this new set of challenges.

We decided that we were both ready. We had always envisioned having children together, and we felt equipped to cope with whatever challenges might come with adoption. We made contact with David J. Radis, a prominent adoption attorney who had offices in Century City. After about three weeks, he located a potential birth mother for us, a Native American woman in her twenties who lived in the Palm Springs area who was pregnant and hoped to offer her baby for adoption. The young woman already had one baby, and David, the lawyer, had been in contact with leaders of her tribe, who might be helpful in facilitating the adoption.

Barbara and I were very excited at the prospect, and we got to work with all of the necessary preparation. We arranged for the young woman to stay in an apartment in Koreatown when it was time to deliver. We were in contact with a hospital in the San Fernando Valley where she would deliver. We began making payments to the lawyer for him to distribute to support her for the remainder of her pregnancy.

Of course, we knew the adoption wasn't a sure thing. By California law, the birth mother would have up to two years after the adoption to change her mind and reclaim the child. Still, we had every indication that this mother was sincere. We were so confident that the adoption would happen that we started sharing the news with friends and relatives, some of whom even threw a baby shower for us. After our years of struggling with infertility, we both felt joyful and eager as we prepared a nursery for the baby and shared our anticipation of the new addition to our family.

When the birth mother came to Los Angeles shortly before her due date, we visited her at the apartment we had rented for her. We found her happily watching MTV, then still in its early years.

Then, just a couple of days before her due date, the lawyer phoned me.

"I'm sorry to be calling with bad news," he said. "We need to stop this process."

The birth mother's relative had been in touch with him, demanding thousands of dollars in additional payments—a bad sign. "I've been in this business long enough to know that this a red flag," he said.

I hung up and shared the news with Barbara. Time stood still. We were devastated. After the weeks and months of eager anticipation, we plunged into mourning. We quietly put the gifts away. We halted our preparations of the nursery. The trauma and agony were overwhelming. It felt like we were at a continuous funeral, going through deep mourning.

In need of a respite from the pain and disappointment,

we decided to get away for a few days. We drove for the weekend to Dana Point, just south of Newport Beach, where we stayed in a hotel overlooking the Pacific Ocean. We spent two days and nights there, feeling sad, holding each other, talking, crying, and discussing how we might move forward. Painful as it was, we both came to a sort of resolve: maybe it just wasn't meant to be.

Just a week later, back home in Los Angeles, I was lying in bed when I heard Barbara screaming and crying from the bathroom. "Oh my God!" she said. "I can't believe it!"

"What?" I asked. "What's wrong?"

She came in, waving a home pregnancy test. "I'm pregnant!"

All this time, as we made preparations for the adoption, we had continued with infertility treatments, but they had never shown any signs of working. Until now. We were both in disbelief. I told Barbara to try repeating the test, just to be sure. She did, and we eagerly waited a minute or so for the result. Again, it turned up positive.

We stood there in disbelief. In just a few days, we had gone from the bottom of the bottom to the highest of highs. I felt like God was watching over us.

I was with Barbara for every step of her pregnancy, accompanying her to every doctor visit at UCLA. I was so devoted that her doctor once teased me for it, telling me he had rarely had a husband insist on accompanying his wife to every appointment. I didn't mean to be overbearing. Barbara and I were very close, and also, after our struggles with infertility, we were both so full of gratitude and excitement that we wanted to share the experience.

Barbara loved being pregnant. In the last weeks of her pregnancy, we would sit together on the sofa in our Pico-Robertson apartment. She would balance a glass of water on her abdomen and watch the movement as the fetus shifted around in her uterus.

Then came the day we had been eagerly anticipating. Around 4 a.m. on January 7, 1991, Barbara woke me up. Her water had broken. "Time to go," she told me.

We were well prepared, with a suitcase packed, so I grabbed it and, in the predawn darkness, we made our way down the steps and into the car. With Barbara in the passenger seat, I steered west on Wilshire Boulevard toward UCLA Medical Center. As I tried to focus on the road, Barbara held my right hand on her belly. I could feel the contractions coming every few minutes.

When we checked in at the hospital, a receptionist directed us to a birthing room. Barbara had chosen her own music to keep her relaxed and soothed during the labor. We listened to it as her contractions grew closer and stronger. After five hours of labor, I saw the baby's head start to emerge with a full head of dark hair. I ran out to alert a nurse: "The baby's here!"

At last, the doctor handed me a beautiful baby girl and gave me a pair of scissors so I could cut the umbilical cord. I felt overwhelming joy. I was so immersed in the experience, so connected to Barbara and to this new human being, that I didn't stop to consider the full span of my life, how it was practically miraculous that I had survived my own childhood, and now—four decades and nearly seven thousand miles from Hatiet Bergen—I was holding my own infant daughter, the beginning of a new generation.

I stayed with Barbara and the baby at the hospital for three nights as she recovered. (The baby had some trouble latching on to breastfeed early on, so they kept Barbara and the baby the extra days.) We had known from an ultrasound that she would be a girl. We wanted a name starting with "J," and we settled on Jessica. Her middle name, Betty, was to honor Barbara's great-aunt, who was born in Russia in 1898 and immigrated to the United Stated through Ellis Island in 1908. The sister of Barbara's maternal grandmother, Aunt Betty was a businesswoman who owned a lingerie store in Greenwich, Connecticut, and was deeply devoted to her extended family, though she never married or had children of her own.

I felt ready to be a father and grateful for the little family we were building.

We wanted to have another child, and we assumed we would have to undergo infertility treatments again. Before we began discussing the options, Barbara called me at work one afternoon in the summer of 1992.

"Ed," she told me, "you need to come home." She wouldn't tell me why. When I arrived, Barbara shared the news with me: she was pregnant again. The two of us, along with baby Jessica, danced around the apartment in celebration.

On the morning of April 28,1993, Barbara told me at six-thirty a.m. that it was time to head to the hospital. Later that morning, she gave birth to a boy we named Jason.

Circumcision had been a part of the culture I grew up with, and I had a strong feeling that I wanted to be present for my son's circumcision. It wasn't a religious impulse as much as a strong instinct, maybe a deep-seated cultural need. I wasn't sure what I wanted to do—hold the baby, perhaps, or simply be there. I was disappointed when the doctor insisted on performing the circumcision without my presence. I wasn't sure what the conflict was, but I was so tired and so elated to have my son that I decided it wasn't a battle I needed to fight that day. Still, I had some lingering sadness that I hadn't been a part of it.

IN MOST WAYS, MY CHILDREN'S EARLY YEARS COULDN'T HAVE been more different from mine. I had grown up in relatively crude conditions, in a mud hut surrounded by extended family, with only loose boundaries separating households. Jessica and Jason grew up half a block from Beverly Hills, one of the most affluent communities on the planet. It wasn't the fanciest upbringing—we lived in a two-bedroom unit of a four-plex, hardly a mansion—but they never lacked for food, they had loving parents, and they went to good schools. When they were very young, Jason adored his older sister, following her around the house and wanting to do whatever she was doing.

We were a typical Los Angeles family: we spent a lot of time with our kids, doing fun and educational activities. We enrolled them in various enrichment classes, and visited the zoo and Disneyland on weekends. We went on hikes, camping trips, and other family journeys. Barbara and I had dreamed of being parents together, and we cherished the time with our growing family.

While our four-person family was smaller than the sprawling tribal unit of my childhood, our children did have proximity to Barbara's parents, who were loving grandparents. They also had cousins, and Barbara's close childhood friend had a son the same age as Jason who was like a quasi-cousin. The extended family made a habit of gathering for the Jewish holidays, primarily Passover and Hanukkah.

I FREQUENTLY TOLD THE CHILDREN STORIES ABOUT MY SCHOOLING and how I came to the United States. They were aware of my background. I told them about how I grew up, my house, the stories my grandmother would tell me. It was difficult for them to imagine. When I told them how I had grown up tending to sheep and camels, how I would wake up early to take care of the chickens, they reacted as if I had told them that I came from outer space.

Barbara and I had decided together to raise our children as Jews. According to Jewish law, having a Jewish mother made them Jewish. We didn't want to confuse them, and in any case, I wasn't a practicing Muslim. They both understood from a young age that they were Jewish. This had positive associations for them, though they occasionally asked if we could decorate for Christmas and we had to remind them that it wasn't our holiday.

Our family would join Barbara's parents each year for the Passover Seder, and at Hanukkah each year, Barbara adorned our home with elaborate and beautiful Hanukkah decorations. And they had Jewish cousins, though Barbara's sister and her Israeli-born husband weren't observant.

Our children both started their education at the Westside Jewish Community Center preschool. There, they learned Hebrew songs, they celebrated Shabbat every Friday, they learned about all of the Jewish holidays, and they made Jewish friends.

That was the extent of their Jewish education. They both went on to a public elementary school, and we never enrolled them in a religious school or joined a temple. It simply wasn't a priority.

Of course, Barbara and I had done our spiritual searching, at the Hollywood Church of Religious Science and elsewhere.

I had also done my share of exploring philosophy, regularly checking out books from the library that went as far back as the Greeks. I read how Socrates would confront people in the market and ask them questions. I studied Cicero's wisdom about the ideal society and the role of government. I devoured biographies of accomplished people, admiring how they had struggled through life, overcome challenges, and found success.

With all of that, I hadn't delved into Judaism with any kind of seriousness. Barbara and I didn't talk much about Judaism. I had come to America with my preconceptions about the Middle East—that the Arabs were right and the Israelis were wrong. As my mind and understanding evolved, my heart sided with the Arabs, but the more I came to understand the nuances and history of the conflict, I assumed a more neutral view.

Those political views were separate from my connection with the Jewish religion, which remained somewhat distant—until Jason shared his desire to have a bar mitzvah. Growing up in our part of Los Angeles, with its heavily Jewish population, he had seen older peers go through the process, and at age twelve, he had friends who were beginning preparations for theirs. Even though we hadn't provided him with any kind of formal Jewish education (beyond the JCC preschool), he was—as the son of a Jewish woman—considered a full-fledged Jew, and he wanted to have a bar mitzvah.

We found him a Hebrew tutor, Luna, a neighbor who was friendly with Barbara and was married to an orthodox rabbi. Luna began teaching him Hebrew and some fundamentals of the Jewish religion. Jason went to the lessons eagerly and enjoyed them.

Barbara decided that the best place for Jason to have his

bar mitzvah was the Chabad Russian Immigrant Synagogue in the Fairfax District, not far from where her parents lived. Both sides of her family had come from Russia, Latvia, and Poland, so she felt a connection there. The rabbi, Naftali Estulin, could not have been more welcoming. He had a large extended family connected to the synagogue, and everyone embraced our family and made Jason feel at home.

At another nearby Chabad center, Chabad of Mt. Olympus (run by Rabbi Estulin's son-in-law, Rabbi Sholom Rodal), Jason began taking Hebrew classes as well as studying Torah and learning about the portion of the Torah he would be chanting at his bar mitzvah. For five months, I accompanied him to nearly every class, driving him after school to the synagogue, which was about five miles from our house. Often on the drive home, the two of us would discuss what he learned and what he thought about it. In addition to studying what he would need for the bar mitzvah service, he was acquiring a broad education about Judaism: Jewish law, keeping kosher, the holidays. It was the religious school he had never experienced.

When Jason decides that he is going to accomplish something, he usually succeeds. In just a few months, he mastered the material, chanting his Torah portion in Hebrew as well as the Haftarah, a selection from the Jewish books of Prophets.

Sitting in on the classes, I gradually became enthralled by everything he was learning. Hebrew and Arabic have many similarities, so it wasn't difficult for me to pick up the Biblical Hebrew. Still, I tried to step back and maintain my role as an observer because I wanted my son to have his own experience, not to feel like I was encroaching on his. Along the way, though, I was absorbing much of what he was learning, and found it all compelling and fascinating.

The bar mitzvah, on May 6, 2006, was a beautiful experience. I felt proud of my son and touched and moved by the many friends and relatives who came to the synagogue that Saturday morning to support Jason and our family.

The rabbi made me feel comfortable and included. He had me stand on the *bimah*, the pulpit, along with Jason, my father-in-law, and the other men, and I wore a *tallit*, a prayer shawl. Barbara's father was called for an *aliyah*, a blessing over the Torah. I had little understanding of the carefully orchestrated protocol of the Shabbat morning service. I assumed that others were participating because they understood Hebrew while I didn't. The rabbi was diplomatic and kind, telling me just to watch and not to worry about anything.

Only years later did I realize that the rabbi was excluding me from participating in the service because I wasn't Jewish. At the time it didn't bother me. (As they say, ignorance is bliss.) In any case, I was moved by the beauty of the service, and the way my son was able to demonstrate what he had learned, and I felt the depth and power of this ancient tradition that he was a part of.

As I watched, I also felt a longing to be part of it myself.

Three weeks later, we continued the celebration with a party at Temple Beth Am, the Conservative synagogue close to our house. Barbara spent countless hours planning and preparing. She decorated the ballroom beautifully. More than one hundred and twenty people joined us, including relatives who came from San Francisco, Connecticut, Florida, and some friends from my Jon Douglas Company days. We had hired a DJ, who included all the usual bar mitzvah party fun and games. We danced in circles to "Hava Nagila;" we held Jason up on a chair; the kids played games on the dance floor. It was a wonderful and joyous time for Jason, Jessica, Barbara, and me.

It was also the first time I had set foot in Temple Beth Am. I had no inkling that it would come to be such a significant part of my life.

———— ⊷⊶ ————

AFTER THAT, I STARTED READING MORE ABOUT JUDAISM, DOING my own exploration. At first, my inquiries were fairly tentative, but then I came to a realization that changed my perspective and sent me in a new direction. I began to think about my own mortality. I had learned along the way that a non-Jew could not be buried in a Jewish cemetery. The more I pondered that idea, the harder it was for me to imagine being separated from Barbara in death. It pained me to think that we could not be buried side-by-side.

I was clear in my mind: I wanted to spend eternity with my wife. I wanted my soul to be Jewish. That initial notion germinated and grew to become a deeply held feeling, eventually leading me to another realization. One morning I woke up and made an announcement to Barbara.

"I've been giving it a lot of thought," I told her. "And I think I want to be Jewish."

It wasn't a desire that I ever expected to have. When I was younger, I never imagined that one day I might want to become a Jew. When I married Barbara, we had discussed the possibility of my conversion to Judaism, but it wasn't something I desired then. I didn't see the need, and Barbara has never been a person to try to talk someone into something they're not ready for.

When our children came along, I never questioned that

they ought to be raised as Jews. But me? When I began considering the notion, I could not ignore it. Perhaps it was more than wanting to be buried next to my wife. Maybe what I was seeking was a sense of belonging to something larger than myself or my family—a feeling that had eluded me since I left my village for middle school. The more time I spent away from Libya, the less I felt connected to the country or to anyone I had known there. For years, I had been on a search—for what, I did not know. Now I felt that I knew, that Judaism had been what I was searching for in my life.

Barbara had listened to me ponder the idea over the years, but never pressured me. Now, hearing the words, she looked at me, smiled, and gave me a hug.

"I always knew this would come," she said, with tears of joy streaming down her face.

It was one thing to realize I wanted to be a Jew. Figuring out how was another matter. Barbara set to work on that, at first hoping to find an easy route—a "drive-by" convertion that would allow me to become Jewish instantly, the way certain chapels in Las Vegas will marry a couple for a small fee, no questions asked. We quickly learned that there is no such thing—at least not with any credibility. Besides, I wanted a more mainstream approach that would give me not just credentials, but a process that would be valuable and meaningful.

I considered an orthodox conversion, but learned that the process would be lengthy and perhaps more stringent than I felt I needed or desired. It was also important to both of us that Barbara take classes along with me, since she had never had her own in-depth Jewish education, and wanted to seize the opportunity to do her own learning. I looked into the Reform movement, but that struck me as too liberal for my leanings and way of thinking. That left Conservative Judaism, but we needed to find a way in. Barbara remembered that a tenant and neighbor of ours, from a decade earlier, Shawn Fields-Meyer, had become a rabbi, and she tracked her down to inquire about how to approach conversion. Rabbi Fields-Meyer recommended a program at the University of Judaism (which later became American Jewish University), an eighteen-month primer in the religion called the Louis and Judith Miller Introduction to Judaism Program, then directed by Rabbi Neil Weinberg.

Barbara and I enrolled together in the program, which was taught by Rabbi Michael Gotlieb of Congregation Kehillat Ma'arav in Santa Monica. The year and a half felt like a second honeymoon, an opportunity to take an adventure together as a couple and explore territory that was new and fascinating to both of us.

For one session our group visited the home of a couple, Joe and Marizon Nimoy, so that we could witness firsthand the practicalities of running a kosher kitchen. They showed us how to separate dishes and cutlery for meat and dairy, which ingredients are and are not allowed in the house, and—biggest of all—how to change the kitchen to prepare for Passover, when no bread or leavened product can come into the house. They were lovely people, and though Marizon herself had converted to Judaism, managing a kosher kitchen seemed second-nature to her. I felt inspired and she helped me not to feel overwhelmed by the prospect of running a kosher home.

We spent many Shabbat mornings at Temple Beth Am, the synagogue near our home where we had hosted Jason's bar mitzvah party. There, we attended the Shabbat morning minyan called BAIT Tefillah, then run by Rabbi Perry Netter. I found him to be bright, warm, and accepting, and the congregants were welcoming and knowledgeable. One congregant in particular, Marshall Kramer, greeted us warmly, generously assisting us getting acquainted with the shul and the order of services. I felt at home almost immediately, and those factors, combined with the synagogue's proximity to my home, made it highly appealing. So, I returned on another Saturday morning, and soon found myself becoming a regular.

One thing that radically changed my life was Shabbat. I had never experienced anything like a traditional Shabbat. It was such a simple idea but had such a profound impact. I found it difficult to believe how much goodness came into my life just from the practice of setting aside one day a week for myself and my family, without interruptions from telephones or television or radio or any of the things that distract us all week. Shabbat was a way of resetting myself emotionally. It was like experiencing a rebirth every week, a chance for introspection and fresh perspective.

Most of the other participants in the class were couples preparing to get married. I was the oldest potential convert in the group, and certainly the only one from a Muslim background.

As I learned more and more about Judaism, I began to experience an unanticipated sense of déjà vu. The more I learned, the more I recognized echoes of my childhood.

In class, we learned about the Jewish practice of adorning a doorway with a *mezuzah*, the small parchment scrolls inscribed with certain Hebrew passages from the Torah. That reminded me of a practice back in Hatiet Bergen, where it was common to place an amulet in the entrance to a house as a form of protection against scorpions and snakes. Usually, it consisted of written passages from the Quran wrapped in palm leaves. This wasn't a common Muslim practice but was typical in our area.

And then there was the language. All over the Arab world, people speak in Arabic, but, as in any other language, there are many dialects, each with its own colloquialisms. When I was growing up, in our village and our local area people used certain words and phrases that aren't commonly used in Arabic. I never understood why.

When I started learning Hebrew and studying Torah in the original Hebrew I began to recognize certain words and phrases from my childhood. *Chamira*, a Hebrew word for leavened products that is mentioned in a blessing tradition-ally said before Passover, was the same word I remembered from childhood. The words of a popular nursery rhyme that parents would sing in my village while tossing an infant in the air and then catching him was called *beh jebar*, similar to the Hebrew word *yitgaber*, "may he be and grow strong." A bar of crushed, dried dates was called *daboose*, echoing *davash*, the Hebrew word for honey.

The more I learned, the more connections I discovered. A blessing I read in the prayer book every week praised those who offer *"fat l'orchim,"* "bread to the wayfarers," using a word very close to *f'tat*, the flat bread my mother used to make in her mud oven. Exodus 21:25 includes the phrase *k'via tachat k'via*, "a burn for a burn," a parallel to *kawi*, the healing-by-burning practice I was subjected to as a child. It may have originated in the days of the prophet Isaiah (Isaiah 6:1-7) when one of the angels *(serafim)* placed a live coal from the altar on his lips as a way to remove guilt and atone for sins. There was even an Israeli city with ancient roots, Bnei Brak, whose name was reminiscent of my childhood city, Brak.

And more: I learned a Biblical phrase that Jews say in the morning while putting on *tefillin* that three times repeats the word "*arastikh*," "I will betroth." It reminded me of *a'rrassa*, the Arabic word for the weeklong celebration of a wedding. This practice also shed light on something I had never previously understood: why the Islamic custom is for a man to repeat the phrase, "I divorce you" three times for the dissolution of marriage to be final.

I began to wonder how these similarities were possible. I could only conclude that at some point people who knew Biblical Hebrew had made their way from Palestine, maybe from Jerusalem, to our part of the Libyan desert. What else could explain it? I would hear these phrases or read them in the text of the Torah and then smile and laugh to myself as I remembered similar words from my childhood. Perhaps hundreds or even thousands of years ago, before Islam, a Jew traveled from the land of Israel or from Egypt to the Fezzan region of Libya and later had to renounce Judaism and take on Islam. Fezzan was home to the great Garamantes Empire from the fifth century BCE to the fifth century CE. Perhaps the Garamantes were Israelites who escaped Egypt by the time of—or even before—the events of the Exodus.

When I remembered my maternal grandmother, my Jida Gazalla, with whom I had such a close bond, I began to think she had had a Jewish soul. She preached acceptance of all kinds of people—a far more open attitude than was common in Libyan society. She had an ease with life and with tradition that exuded a sense of wisdom and calm. She was a natural nomadic soul, a prophetess in human psychology.

For all of these reasons, I began to think of my Jewish journey not as an exploration of new territory, but as a return to something that may have been buried deep inside myself.

Rabbi Neal Weinberg, who was running the Introduction to Judaism program, encouraged students to affiliate with a synagogue. Some participants had already settled on a synagogue or they connected to one through their spouses or fiancés—or their families. Others had begun the process at a synagogue and had rabbis who had referred them. I had neither a rabbi nor a synagogue, but I had attended Rabbi Netter's service at Temple Beth Am several times. I felt comfortable there and enjoyed his presence. So I made an appointment to ask if he would be willing to serve as the sponsoring rabbi for my conversion.

Barbara came along for my first meeting with him. After some initial conversation, Rabbi Netter asked me the most important and relevant question: "Why do you want to become a Jew?"

I opened my mouth to reply, but nothing came out. I felt overwhelmed with emotion. All at once I felt joy, longing, sadness, relief, excitement, and love. I felt hope for my future and connection to my past. Rabbi Netter didn't know any of that. All he saw was a silent, tongue-tied man sitting across from him. As the rabbi waited for my answer, and Barbara sat beside me holding my hand, I simply wept, expressing my inner joy.

The rabbi smiled. "It's okay," he said gently. "I understand. You pass."

I sat there for fifteen minutes or so, overwhelmed, silent, and shedding tears. I had gone through my life in so many ways alone, without my family, without my native culture, without feeling a part of something larger than myself. And now I had found it, and at the same time, I had come to understand feelings I had carried all my life. There was a thread connecting the past with the present. I was over-whelmed with the goodness of it all. It was impossible to express what this meant to me.

I felt that same tangle of feelings, only more intensely, on the morning when I finally completed my conversion process and appeared before the *beit din*, the rabbinical court that was required to approve my conversation. The panel consisted of three elderly rabbis, two of them with walkers, all probably in their nineties. They asked me a few questions to test my knowledge, but then one of them asked the same question Rabbi Netter had posed: Why do you want to be Jewish? I should have been prepared, especially after my earlier experience. But once again, I felt the emotions well up, and again I just wept.

The *beit din* gave me approval for conversation. The next step, to make it official, was for me to emerge in the *mikveh*, the ritual bath. One of the rabbis led me to the *mikveh*, in a special room at the university. As I recited the blessings and submerged my body into the waters of the *mikveh*, I shed tears. I felt truly transformed, like a new person. At the same time, I felt that I had returned to something from my past. I felt connected—to my family, to my past, to God, to the Jewish people. Finally, I had what I had been searching for all my life.

⟁

I WAS DETERMINED TO BE NOT JUST A JEW, BUT AN ACTIVE AND committed Jew. Barbara and I began to celebrate Shabbat, both at home and in synagogue. She lit the candles at sundown. I went to services as much as I could—often for Friday night Kabbalat Shabbat services, again Saturday morning, and for mincha, the service on Saturday afternoon. For the first six months I simply listened and watched. I considered myself a "Jew-in-training." It seemed that nearly everyone else was comfortable and well versed. (Later I would learn the truth, that congregants brought a diverse array of background and knowledge levels.)

Besides Judaism's beautiful and meaningful rituals and practices, I was drawn to its understanding of human nature, and, in particular, its recognition that human beings are fallible and imperfect, that we often fall short, but there is always room for forgiveness and improvement. I also loved the Jewish view that we should learn to accept and live with doubt and its view that humans are born with both the inclination for good, *yetzer hatov*, and inclination for bad, *yetzer hara*. The culture I came from was in many ways so harsh and unforgiving that I found beauty and a sense of relief in the idea that falling short was only human.

I also gained a deep appreciation and love for Israel. Of course, I had the perspective I had brought from my upbringing. I was raised to believe that Jews had illegally occupied Palestine, stealing the land that belonged to Arabs and Muslims. Back in Libya, Israel didn't appear in our textbooks for any subject. When I learned history, nobody explained that the Jewish people have deep roots in Israel and in the Arab World, going back thousands of years to biblical times. As far as I had been taught, Zionists were interlopers, outsiders who had stolen land and displaced the indigenous peoples. In the Arab world, the very existence of Israel was viewed as a disaster, an insult that Arabs and Muslims needed to reverse and avenge.

Then there was my father-in-law. Barbara's father, Robert, who was born in Pinsk and immigrated to Palestine as a child. During the War of Independence, he served in the Israeli Air Force. He was based in Jaffa, working in collaboration with an Italian-born doctor who was a chemist. Together they created barrel bombs, crude devices controlled by timers that the Air Force would drop on targets.

After the war, he eventually made his way to the United States and to Los Angeles, but he never strayed from his deeply held love of Israel and his support for the Jewish state. Certainly, we had our discussions over the years, but from the time I connected with Barbara, I accepted Israel's legitimacy and never questioned its right to exist.

When I decided to convert to Judaism, my primary motivations were positive: the connection I felt, the sense of community, the beauty of Shabbat and the holidays. One unexpected benefit of converting to Judaism was that my new religion had a softening effect. I saw more clearly my tendency to be confrontational, to act with anger and resentment. Judaism is a religion and culture that embraces argument. Indeed, the entire Talmud is a record of disagreements and debates among generations of wise rabbis. But it also has laws about how to disagree. The rabbis of the Talmud famously describe *machloket l'shem shamayim,* a "disagreement for the sake of heaven."

Judaism, I learned, isn't about being right and proving the other person wrong. It's a process of acquiring knowledge—about yourself and about the world around you.

THE MORE I LEARNED ABOUT JUDAISM, THE MORE CONNECTION I felt toward Israel.

In some ways, my attachment was intellectual and practical. I came to feel very strongly that Israel is vital to the survival of the Jewish people. If Israel did not exist, Jews would be stateless people, second-class citizens, no matter where they lived.

Over time, I became transformed into something I would never have imagined becoming when I was a teenager in Libya: an avowed defender of Israel and a passionate Zionist. The more passionate I felt about Israel, and the more emotionally invested, the more I wanted to visit the country and experience it in person. In the spring of 2012, Barbara and I made plans to take a trip there in the following November. She got to work planning our itinerary to include visits to her various Israeli friends and to Kibbutz Beit Alfa, where she had spent time during the Yom Kippur War.

As it turned out, we had chosen a difficult time to visit. That autumn Hamas launched more than one hundred rockets at Israel from Gaza, and on November 14, Israel responded by killing the chief of the Gaza military wing of Hamas, Ahmed Jabari. Those events escalated into a major Israeli campaign, Operation Pillar of Defense, aimed at permanently halting Hamas's rocket attacks from Gaza on Israel.

As the date of our departure neared, Barbara and I monitored the headlines with great apprehension, wondering whether it was wise to put our safety in jeopardy by visiting a country in the midst of a major military conflict. We consulted with friends from our synagogue who had spent time there, seeking advice about the right thing to do. Some of them suggested rescheduling the trip, if not for safety's sake, simply so we could visit at a later date, after things calmed down. Several relatives also encouraged us to postpone the trip.

That didn't sit right with me. We had made a commitment. "How can we not go?" I asked Barbara. "How could we abandon our family in a time of need?" Jewish soldiers were fighting to protect our people. And we couldn't make a vacation trip?

Ultimately, we came to the joint decision that this wasn't

simply a vacation; it was an opportunity to make a statement—to express our love and support for Israel, and to
demonstrate what it meant to be committed Jews and Zionists. We agreed to make the trip as planned.

As the day of our departure neared, Barbara warned me
to be prepared for El Al's meticulous passenger screening.
Surely the Israeli security personnel would take special note
of a passenger with an Arabic surname who was born in Libya.
On the day of our flight, we arrived early at the international
terminal at Los Angeles International Airport, prepared for
a lengthy interrogation. But when we got to security, the
agent glanced at my passport, looked up at me, then asked
only a few general questions and sent me through. The entire
encounter lasted no longer than two minutes. I smiled at
Barbara, whose surprised expression said, "That's it?" She
seemed almost disappointed by the lack of drama.

Knowing the Gaza conflict was raging, we prepared for
the worst, but as it turned out, our timing was fortuitous. Our
flight arrived on the late afternoon of Wednesday, November
21, 2012. As we touched down at Ben Gurion International
Airport, I was filled with emotion, overwhelmed by my
unlikely journey from my village in Libya to this visit as
a Jew to Israel. We soon learned that just minutes before
our arrival, the fighting in Gaza had halted: Hillary Clin-
ton, the U.S. secretary of state, and Mohamed Kamel Amr,
the Egyptian foreign minister, had issued a joint statement
announcing a cease-fire.

When we arrived at our hotel, the Dan Panorama in Tel
Aviv, I noticed a number of signs in the lobby instructing
guests what to do and where to go in case of an air-raid
siren. That gave me pause and reminded me that everything
I had been reading and watching on the news from home

was now all too real. But I was determined not to let that interfere with our visit.

Barbara was exhausted from the long flight, so she went directly to sleep in the hotel. But I felt energized and eager to see the country, so I went for a walk through the streets of Tel Aviv and Jaffa. I was amazed. The boulevards were full of life: parents pushing children in strollers, people walking their dogs, elderly people chatting on benches. People were going on with their lives. The cease-fire had just been declared, and I felt completely safe—and at home. I saw people of all shades—black, brown, white. As I wandered the streets for a few hours, Israel became a different place in my mind, a stark contrast with its portrayal by the media in the United States and across the world.

During our ten days of travel, I felt joy and gratitude at practically every moment, as I took in every view and encounter. I savored the view of Jerusalem, with its golden stones, at sunset. We prayed the Friday night service, Kabbalat Shabbat, at Jerusalem's Great Synagogue, where Sephardic and Ashkenazic services took place simultaneously in different parts of the building. On my first visit to the Kotel, the Western Wall, I stood on a Thursday morning, wrapped in my *tallit* and touching the massive, ancient stones as tears ran down my cheeks. We returned for a Shabbat morning service where I received an *aliyah* and afterward locals invited us into their home for a Kiddush lunch. That afternoon we walked from the Old City into West Jerusalem, to meet friends in the neighborhood of Katamon. In Tsfat I immersed in an outdoor *mikveh* of cold spring water. In Tel Aviv we visited the apartment building where Barbara's father had lived in his teenage years, recalling the stories he had often shared of his life there in the 1940s.

We visited old sites: Caesarea, Beit She'an, Masada. We saw places significant to more modern Jewish and Israeli history: Latrun, Yad Vashem, Ammunition Hill, the ammunition factory beneath a bakery in Rehovot. We visited Ben Gurion's residence in Tel Aviv and marveled at the cramped, modest space, with walls full of books and souvenirs from heads of states. We saw the Lebanese border at Rosh HaNikra and the Syrian border in the Golan Heights.

I did my best to focus on the present moment, to take in every place, every conversation, every experience. But at the same time, I couldn't help but travel to my past. I reflected on my childhood, when I knew nothing about Israel or any of these places, only that a *Yahudi* was the worst thing to be, and that it was our duty as Arabs and Muslims to drive the Jews out. I had come such a long way from my origins to this moment, when I felt not only comfortable, but completely at home. Israel wasn't just a place I could appreciate and admire, it felt like the place where I belonged. It was mine.

From that time, on, I began to take notice of a prayer we recite every Shabbat morning in synagogue just after the reading of the Torah and Haftarah: the Prayer for the State of Israel. I hadn't given it much thought before, but now I started saying it each week with full intention: "Bless the land with peace, and its inhabitants with lasting joy."

Occasionally as I said those words, I would think back to my fifteen-year-old self, on that hot June afternoon on the streets of Sebha during the Six-Day War. And I said an extra prayer of gratitude to God for carrying me on this remarkable journey to myself.

CHAPTER 8

Living with Ease

⸻❦⸻

When Jessica was eight years old, in elementary school, she began struggling academically. At first, her teachers suspected she had ADHD (Attention Deficit Hyperactivity Disorder), but then she struggled with learning difficulties, particularly in mathematics.

We found that her school wasn't particularly focused on helping children like her. It was easier to label them and try to fix them. While it may have been convenient for the school, we didn't feel that a diagnosis helped Jessica. Instead, it created a stigma. Instead of thinking of her struggles as challenges they could help her understand and cope with in positive ways, they came to see her as a problem to be solved. That escalated as she went through middle school and on to high school.

For high school, she attended Summit View School, a therapeutic school aimed at helping children with learning disabilities. At the time, I thought Jessica was enjoying herself, but later I learned that she was a victim of bullying. Even though the school was supposedly designed to serve students like Jessica, her teachers and counselors failed to provide the emotional support she required. After her graduation, she faced depression and became socially isolated.

She spent two years at Santa Monica College in the cosmetology program, then took a very difficult and comprehensive six-hour state licensing exam, passing it on her first attempt. Then she took a three-week recess to recuperate. When we asked her to search for employment, she was reluctant and she mostly stayed home, not venturing out to the world much.

As a parent, I sometimes feel torn. Of course, I want to listen to my daughter, to offer support and for our home to be a place of comfort and security. On the other hand, when home becomes a refuge from truly stepping out into the world, into life, then there are professional healthcare services to help deal with these issues. As parents, we want to help, but often it's difficult to know the best way to do so.

What helped us the most is the National Alliance on Mental Illness (NAMI), a support and advocacy group that has chapters across the country. One of Jessica's therapists suggested that we connect with NAMI, and once we did, Barbara and I started feeling much less alone. We made connections with other parents and relatives of people coping with mental and psychological challenges. Many of them had far more experience with these issues than we did.

NAMI offers a twelve-week course open to anyone in the life of a loved one with mental illness. Each week the class covers a different issue: medications and their side effects, the biology of the brain, coping with grief and other emotions, how to talk with psychiatrists and other healthcare providers. It also covers how to take care of yourself; if you neglect your own health and well-being, it's difficult to help your loved one. If you don't have the tools to cope with a relative's mental illness, it's easy to become bogged down or sick yourself, or to be sucked into the vortex of the loved one's struggles.

We also took part in some of NAMI's support groups, which helped us in profound ways to understand Jessica, to cope with our own struggles, and to know how to support our daughter. Parents and other relatives shared information about interacting with the healthcare system, managing legal issues, and the specifics of diagnoses, such as bipolar disorder and schizophrenia. Sometimes what's most helpful is the emotional support: "I understand your pain. I'm sorry you're having to deal with that right now."

Since I have a background in science, I also took it upon myself to research her challenges and try to understand what she was coping with. The difficulty of that kind of investigation is that the more you know, the less you know. In other words, the more knowledge you gain about the subject, the more you realize the amount of information you are unfamiliar with. Still, in my experience, education is the best way to find understanding, relief, and potential recovery for your loved one.

Gaining knowledge also helped us to become advocates to deal with the stigmas and stereotypes surrounding mental illness. In short, people fundamentally misunderstand what mental illness is. When a person has a physical ailment—heart trouble or a broken leg, for example—friends and coworkers often visit in the hospital, bringing flowers or food. But when you have a child in the hospital with mental illness, nobody visits. When the child returns home from the hospital, nobody calls. It's complete silence. Most people simply don't know what to do or say.

When a person has a diagnosis of mental illness, those who know tend to see everything the person does through that lens. If a typical person is yelling or screaming, we assume that they're in a bad mood. But if someone with schizophrenia or bipolar disorder does the same things, most people attribute it to the diagnosis.

As I learned, not only did I gain insight into my daughter's struggles, but I also came to understand myself better. I see myself as a survivor. From a young age, I had to fend for myself without the kind of guidance and support that many children enjoy. That meant I spent much of my youth on high alert, in fight-or-flight mode. Living in that state, I lost connection with my feelings, or at least they became a jumble that was difficult to decipher. Sometimes I didn't know if I felt angry or upset, sad or anxious.

Being a scientist helped. I relied on science and rationality to make sense of things. When Jessica was first facing her challenges, I would think in terms of finding ways to fix her. Over time, I learned to accept her the way she is and ask her how I can help. I encourage her and try to support her, but I avoid the impulse to view my daughter as a problem to be solved. I see the same transition in people who come to the NAMI Family-to-Family sessions I teach a few times a year. People come looking for a cure, a solution, but within a few weeks, they learn about acceptance and advocacy.

⸕⸕⸕

AS I STRUGGLED TO UNDERSTAND HOW THE MIND AND BODY relate, I began exploring mindfulness and meditation. Years earlier, around the time I arrived in Los Angeles, I had listened to Alan Watts, who frequently spoke on Pacifica Radio about Buddhism and striving to be in the present. When the mind and body are in sync, he taught, you can be attentive to the present moment. Time stops. Mental anguish falls away.

In those days, I listened to what he had to say, but I didn't fully integrate his ideas into my life.

Then around the Spring of 2012, I began reading more about mindfulness meditation. I read the writings of Jack Kornfield, who has been teaching about Buddhist ideas since the 1970s. Barbara and I started attending a Sunday sitting at a mindfulness center in Santa Monica called InsightLA, founded by a wonderful, civic-minded Dharma teacher, Trudy Goodman. Every Sunday, about sixty people meditate together for about forty-five minutes. I have found it to be a beautiful and helpful way to cope with challenges that arise in life. Making meditation a regular habit makes life less overwhelming. It has helped me to realize that many of the matters that occupy us are fleeting: they come and go. I might arrive at the session feeling concerned about something, but after a while, it fades, replaced by another thought.

The more I learn about mindfulness practice, the more I see how it relates directly to Jewish ideas and practices. The Jewish calendar—with its daily, weekly, monthly, and annual cycles for prayers, events, and holidays—serves to remind us to be mindful of the sacredness of every moment. The *mezuzah*, posted on the doorway, is a physical reminder to be mindful of the holiness of space. Havdalah, the ritual that marks the transition from Shabbat to the rest of the week, make us conscious of the distinctive qualities of different days and times. And all of these help to make us mindful of the Divine, of God's presence in our world and in our lives.

It was watching Jessica's struggles that prompted me to delve into mindfulness practice in an effort to offer her some reprieve. Watching her difficulties, I was struggling myself. One way to approach that kind of challenge is to focus on the suffering, on the pain, on the agony. I certainly had my share of those. But that didn't help Jessica and it didn't help me. Focusing on my own pain became overwhelming. What helped was taking a different approach: radical acceptance with lovingkindness and compassion. I told myself: no matter how bad things appear, accept it. That doesn't mean the situation will stay as it is forever, but once you accept the situation and you do not consider yourself as a victim and stuck in it by blaming others, you can move forward and focus on solutions instead of on your pain and your anger.

Looking back, I don't think I ever truly understood myself or knew who I was until I started trying to help Jessica. I have always been grateful to my son, Jason, for guiding me toward Judaism, and bringing me back to what I have come to feel are my deepest roots. And I am thankful to Jessica for helping me to love myself and accept myself the way I am. Before Jessica's challenges emerged, I was overly focused on myself—trying to improve myself, even rehabilitate myself—as if something was broken or missing. Judaism certainly gave me some of what was missing inside. Helping Jessica helped me to accept myself and bring my life into focus and to be a better father to her.

I don't think I would be able to do any of this if I hadn't come to Judaism, the cornerstone of my spiritual life. As I see it, Judaism transported me back to where I belong: I am home. Before, I was searching for answers: in science, in philosophy, in other people's stories. When I fully accepted Judaism, I stopped searching for answers. I became consciously aware and accepting of all my daily life's possibilities with ease.

Epilogue

O f all of my Jewish practices—Shabbat dinner, Torah
study, lighting the Shabbat candles, attending Shabbat
services—one of my favorites happens every morning, as
soon as I open my eyes. The first words I utter are the words
of *Modeh Ani*, the Hebrew prayer that expresses gratitude to
God for our very existence. Judaism has blessings for practically everything we do: blessings over different kinds of
foods, over special occasions and holidays, even for going to
the bathroom. The one I find most meaningful, though, is the
Modeh Ani, which is simply a statement of thanks for waking
up in the morning and being aware of the present moment.

I have every reason to be grateful. It's not difficult to
see that my very existence is a miracle. It never escapes my
mind that three of my siblings died young, that all around
me in childhood lurked death. I have never taken my own
existence for granted. Every breath, every moment seems
precious, a gift.

Nor do I take for granted the remarkable freedoms I enjoy,
choices I didn't have as a child and that I certainly would
have sacrificed if I had returned to Libya.

I am grateful for my ability to reason.

So many people in this world feel locked into the cir-
cumstances they have inherited: the geographical location,
the belief system, the attitudes towards other human beings.

They fall into lives that perpetuate the status quo, never questioning its merit or the possibility of what else might be.

Because I was motivated to excel at science in high school, and then because my mother's death inspired me to direct my energies into my studies, I became a scientist. As such, I understood how to evaluate evidence and come to my own conclusions.

So, my mind was prepared when I arrived at the University of Wisconsin-Madison and started meeting Jewish people. All my life, I had been told that Jews were the monsters I saw in Egyptian propaganda movies, that they were baby killers, that they were awful people, the enemies of Arabs and Muslims.

But then the evidence showed otherwise. Not only were the Jews I met not baby killers, but they were far more loving, accepting, and peaceful than the people I knew back in Libya.

I am grateful to live in the United States and immensely grateful to be an American.

People who were born into the freedom, diversity, and democracy of the United States can easily take those things for granted. Not I. My story of transformation could only have happened here in America.

In America, I encountered people different from me, with different backgrounds, different beliefs, different outlooks. In America, I had the choice to associate with whomever I wanted.

Once I used my ability to reason to conclude that Jews were not the evil people I had been told, America gave me the freedom to seek out connections with Jewish people to learn more about them, to become part of their community. I cannot imagine that happening in any other country.

America offers the remarkable chance for transformation,

the opportunity to become what you want to become. It is an exceptional nation that recognizes, in the words of the Declaration of Independence, that "all men are created equal, that they are endowed by their Creator with certain unalienable Rights, [and] that among these are Life, Liberty, and the Pursuit of Happiness."

No place is perfect. The Founding Fathers had slaves. Racism is awful. We certainly should acknowledge what happened in the past. But it's even more important to recognize the present and the remarkable progress we have made. It's a beautiful country. (See page 175 for a poem I wrote capturing my love for America.)

I'm grateful to be a Jew. Being a Jew has always been— and still is—an adventurous and risky business. But it comes with tremendous benefits: experiencing and living my free will and charting my desired destiny in contributing to the world in a way to enhance it for all humanity. I benefit from the deeds of people before me, and I hope my deeds will bear fruits in coming generations.

Looking back, I have endured many risks, challenges, and tribulations. Among the hardest was leaving my profession, chemical engineering, which I considered my identity. All of these experiences have led me to my bravest decision yet: becoming a Jew.

Judaism has given meaning to my life. It has brought me into a community of depth and purpose. It has also helped me open my heart and mind to the world around me and heightened my awareness that we are all bound together— not just Jews, but all of humanity.

Before I embraced Judaism, I was far more self-absorbed, far less conscious of building relationships with others. I simply didn't appreciate people. Besides my connections with immediate family, I saw most relationships as temporary and transactional. Because of that, I missed out on many friendships and connections.

That attitude stemmed in large part from the culture I came from, in which individuals were preoccupied with surviving and getting through the day. They didn't have the luxury to think about others, or perhaps just didn't understand the benefits that arise from mutual support and connection with people from cultures or religions different from their own.

Before I began exploring Judaism, I paid little attention to homeless people on the street. If I saw them, I moved on, feeling no obligation or even inclination to offer help. Now I see those people. I understand that they are created in the image of God. I feel the person's predicament, and I do what I can to help.

It is a liberating joy for me to believe that as the human body consists of many organs, small and large, working together in harmony, so does our world comprise all of its inhabitants, of animate and inanimate creatures, interconnected and coexisting for the purpose of all. As the kidney is dependent on the heart and the stomach is dependent on the lungs—and vice versa—so is every creature in our world dependent on every other. When one suffers harm, all suffer harm.

Some people dismiss Judaism—or religion in general—as meaningless or irrelevant to their lives. Even many Jews find the religion to be repetitious, the rituals to be puzzling, the texts to be difficult to relate to. But what I have found is that believing in something larger than myself and accepting a set of values that have been tested and proven helpful for millennia brings all kinds of positive things to my life.

Sometimes reading the stories in the Torah can be painful and difficult. What I have found in my Torah study, though, is that Torah presents human beings as we truly are. Torah presents an unvarnished portrait of humanity. It documents the good and the bad and everything in between. At first, I found these passages troubling, but over time I learned how the sages struggled with these stories over generations. These sagas aren't always meant to show us how to behave. Often the lesson is for us not to repeat the mistakes we're reading about and to struggle for ideals.

I believe strongly in the Jewish idea, rooted in the Torah, that none of us are inherently good or bad people. Each of us has two competing forces within us: a *yetzer hatov*, and a *yetzer hara*—that is, a good inclination and an evil inclination. It's up to each of us to be aware of the potential within us, and to struggle with these inclinations through life.

That idea acknowledges the complexity of our lives and our difficult choices. We have free will to choose—with the full knowledge that we might make the wrong choice. We need to examine why people do good things and why people do evil things. If we're aware of that struggle, it helps us make sense of our lives.

I like to be around happy people. Unhappy people commit fallacious actions. If you're happy and satisfied, you do good things. Whatever I want in my life, I create the space within me for receiving it simply by helping someone else achieve it. If I want a smile on my face, I help someone to smile. If I wanted to climb Mount Everest, I would help another person who wants to achieve the same goal. It is receiving our deeds multiplied by first giving them away!

The truth is, it's usually easier to do bad things. Doing something good is often harder. Even smiling at someone can take effort. It's easier to criticize a person than to praise him.

Over time, I have become a happier, more productive person. I learned to live in this world and embrace the goodness in this world.

I believe in universal consciousness. We're all in it together. The world is energy, and we all have—or are—different levels of energy. We communicate our feelings, our emotions, and our thoughts through our daily deeds, *mitzvot*, in order to do the work of repairing this fractious world—*tikkun olam.*

When we put goodness into the world, it affects the universal consciousness. If we put negative thoughts into the world, it affects it in a different way.

Finally, I'm grateful for the path that my life has taken. I'm grateful for Barbara, for her love and for this unlikely journey that began on a tennis court.

Nearly four decades ago, I left everything I knew for an unfamiliar place, a new culture where I knew almost no one. I thought I would return to build the country of my birth, but my expectations changed.

Three decades ago I reacted with disappointment and anger when I wasn't able to secure work in chemical engineering, the field to which I had devoted many years of hard work. Again, my expectations changed.

Two and a half decades ago, Barbara and I were devastated when our adoption fell through. Just over nine months later, we had a beautiful baby daughter.

What I have learned is that sometimes God has plans for us that we cannot see. Now I thank God every day for the detours my life has taken.

If I had completed my degree at Wisconsin and returned to work in Libya, I would have been lost to the world, in a way, working to support a corrupt regime in a hateful culture.

If I had landed work in my field, I would never have discovered the rich and full life that I have. I wouldn't have found my way to Judaism. I wouldn't have found my way to mindfulness. I wouldn't have found happiness.

Happiness is much more important than money or recognition or accomplishment. At one time in my life, I thought every human being had a limited supply of happiness: if you use it, you lose it. I thought I couldn't replenish it. If I went around smiling, I would lose my reservoir of kindness, so I needed to use it sparingly. But that's silly. You can be happy today, tomorrow, and forever. And the more kind you are, the more kindness comes back to you. It doesn't cost anything.

When I was unhappy with myself, I would criticize other people. I judged people. The happier I became with myself, the more accepting I became of others. My vigilant awareness and reassessing of the outcome of life events and people's actions has become the key to my ability to transform my conditions. I want to put positive energy into the world.

I don't think much about how I want to be remembered. I don't think of death as an end, but as a transformation. For much of my life, I was afraid of dying. But now I think of death as a time to change into a different form of energy. I don't believe that we live only for our human lifespans any more than I believe the planet Earth is the entire universe. Just as I do not know what happened before birth, I also don't know what happens after death, but I don't think it's the end of the story.

Here is what I would want people to say about me: that I was a blessed man who contributed to his world as best he could; that I partook in everything possible; that I did my best to influence the world in a positive way.

All these years later, I still hear the voice of my grandmother: "Your life has been written in the back of your head since your birth," she said. "Just trust yourself and all will end up well." I still feel her presence. I sometimes wonder what she would think of my life now, half a world away from the village where she would lull me to sleep with stories about faraway lands and fantastical characters.

I never heard my grandmother raise her voice. She was always calm, and she counseled others to stay cool, too. Whatever the situation, she would tell people "Don't worry about it. Things will work out. Everything will be okay."

It turns out she was right.

Ed Elhaderi

Our Wedding Vows

*The vows we wrote for our wedding, on December 26, 1980,
as written by Ed (then Abdul) and Barbara Elhaderi.*

---

*Love is the fulfillment of Life; that is, we never can live life
to the fullest unless we are motivated by Love, by a sincere
desire to express unity, harmony, and peace.*

*As the true artist weds himself to the essence of beauty,
imbibing its spirit that he may transmit it to the canvas, so
Barbara and Abdul wed themselves to the essence of Love,
that they may imbibe it and transmit it, give loveliness to all
their life's experiences.*

*Love is fundamental to life, the great and supreme reality.
Love is the highest gift of Heaven, the greatest good on Earth,
and the treasure of all our search.*

*We cannot doubt that God is Love, because hate kills, while
Love renews and restores. Love transmits the essence of life
to everything it touches, awakening within all things an
equal awareness and response. Love is the greatest healing
power there is, and no one feels whole without it.*

*May the joining of our lives be an inspiration to us and all
who our lives touch. May our love be an instrument of peace,
our home a temple of joy, our unity a reminder that we are
all brothers and sisters. May our children remember us for
making life wonderful. May they stand in awe of You, the
God of us all.*

I, Barbara/Abdul, promise you, Barbara/Abdul, to be your wife/husband forever. As your wife/husband, I promise to continue to Love you and to spread our love to others, to seek peace in and with you, for ourselves, for our children, and for our world, and to find joy in and with you and through all the laughter of all that is. And, I promise to be responsible for you forever, because I love you.

Thank you God, for making Abdul and Barbara an instrument of your peace and love. Where there is hatred, let them bring love. Where there is injury, pardon. Where there is doubt, faith. Where there is despair, hope. Where there is darkness, light. Where there is sadness, joy. That they may not so much seek to be consoled, as to console, to be understood, as to understand, to be loved, as to love.

Barbara:/Ed: I promise to be with you and for you; to share my life, my feelings, my hopes, and my experiences with you; to respect your individuality; and to love you. I give you this ring as a symbol of my promise.

For the joy of this occasion; for the meaning of this wedding day; for this important moment in our ever-growing relationship, we thank you for your presence at our wedding!

I Love the USA!

A poem written by the author on January 4, 2004

I traveled many places,
I have seen many faces,
And I chose you.
Your skies are blue,
Your air is fresh,
And I love you.
Your arms are open,
Your smile is warm,
And your conscience is pure.
You nourish and you protect,
You always give,
And you don't expect.
Divinely you are here,
Misery and fear shall disappear.
Trust and faith in you will endure,
You are there time after time
Courageous and sure.
I can't ask more of you,
I am forever grateful
And forever love and protect you.
I love the USA!

Treaty of Tripoli

—⊖⊖⊖—

The Treaty of Tripoli, initiated by President George Washington and approved in 1796 by President John Adams, aimed to protect American commercial ships in the Mediterranean from Barbary pirates. A second treaty, in 1805, established peace and friendship between the United States and Tripoli (Libya).

5th Congress.]   No. 122.   [1st Session.

TRIPOLI.

COMMUNICATED TO THE SENATE, MAY 26, 1797.

UNITED STATES, *May* 26, 1797.

Gentlemen of the Senate:

I lay before you, for your consideration and advice, a treaty of perpetual peace and friendship between the United States of America and the Bey and subjects of Tripoli, of Barbary, concluded, at Tripoli, on the 4th day of November, 1796.

JOHN ADAMS.

•

Treaty of peace and friendship between the United States of America and the Bey and Subjects of Tripoli, of Barbary.

ARTICLE 1. There is a firm and perpetual peace and friendship between the United States of America and the Bey and subjects of Tripoli, of Barbary, made by the free consent of both parties, and guarantied by the most potent Dey and Regency of Algiers.

ART. 2. If any goods belonging to any nation, with which either of the parties is at war, shall be loaded on board of vessels belonging to the other party, they shall pass free, and no attempt shall be made to take or detain them.

ART. 3. If any citizens, subjects, or effects, belonging to either party, shall be found on board a prize vessel, taken from an enemy by the other party, such citizens or subjects shall be set at liberty, and the effects restored to the owners.

ART. 4. Proper passports are to be given to all vessels of both parties, by which they are to be known. And considering the distance between the two countries, eighteen months, from the date of this treaty, shall be allowed for procuring such passports. During this interval the other papers, belonging to such vessels, shall be sufficient for their protection.

Art. 5. A citizen or subject of either party having bought a prize vessel, condemned by the other party, or by any other nation, the certificates of condemnation and bill of sale shall be a sufficient passport for such vessel for one year; this being a reasonable time for her to procure a proper passport.

Art. 6. Vessels of either party, putting into the ports of the other, and having need of provisions or other supplies, they shall be furnished at the market price. And if any such vessel shall so put in, from a disaster at sea, and have occasion to repair, she shall be at liberty to land and re-embark her cargo without paying any duties. But in no case shall she be compelled to land her cargo.

Art. 7. Should a vessel of either party be cast on the shore of the other, all proper assistance shall be given to her and her people; no pillage shall be allowed; the property shall remain at the disposition of the owners; and the crew protected and succored till they can be sent to their country.

Art. 8. If a vessel of either party should be attacked by an enemy, within gun-shot of the forts of the other, she shall be defended as much as possible. If she be in port she shall not be seized on, or attacked, when it is in the power of the other party to protect her. And when she proceeds to sea, no enemy shall be allowed to pursue her from the same port, within twenty-four hours after her departure.

Art. 9. The commerce between the United States and Tripoli; the protection to be given to merchants, masters of vessels, and seamen; the reciprocal right of establishing consuls in each country; and the privileges, immunities, and jurisdictions, to be enjoyed by such consuls, are declared to be on the same footing with those of the most favored nationsre spectively.

Art. 10. The money and presents demanded by the Bey of Tripoli, as a full and satisfactory consideration on his part, and on the part of his subjects, for this treaty of perpetual peace and friendship, are acknowledged to have been received by him previous to his signing the same, according to a receipt which is hereto annexed, except such part as is promised, on the part of the United States, to be delivered and paid by them on the arrival of their consul in Tripoli; of which part a note is likewise hereto annexed. And no pretence of any periodical tribute of further payments is ever to be made by either party.

Art. 11. As the Government of the United States of America is not, in any sense, founded on the Christian religion; as it has in itself no character of enmity against the laws, religion, or tranquillity, of Mussulmen; and, as the said States never entered into any war, or act of hostility againt any Mahometan nation, it is declared by the parties, that no pretext, arrising from religious opinions, shall ever produce an interruption of the harmony existing between the two countries.

Art. 12. In case of any dispute, arising from a violation of any of the articles of this treaty, no appeal shall be made to arms; nor shall war be declared on any pretext whatever. But if the consul, residing at the place where the dispute shall happen, shall not be able to settle the same, an amicable reference shall be made to the mutual friend of the parties, the Dey of Algiers; the parties hereby engaging to abide by his decision. And he, by virtue of his signature to this treaty, engages for himself and successors to declare the justice of the case, according to the true interpretation of the treaty, and to use all the means in his power to enforce the observance of the same.

Signed and sealed at Tripoli, of Barbary, the 3d day of Junad, in the year of the Hegira 1211—corresponding with the 4th day of November, 1796, by

> JUSSOF BASHAW MAHOMET, *Bey.*
> MAMET, *Treasurer.*
> AMET, *Minister of Marine.*
> SOLIMAN KAYA.
> GALEL, *General of the Troops.*
> MAHOMET, *Commander of the City.*
> AMET, *Chamberlain.*
> ALLY, *Chief of the Divan.*
> MAMET, *Secretary.*

Signed and sealed at Algiers, the 4th day of Argill, 1211—corresponding with the 3d day of January, 1797, by

> HASSAN BASHAW, *Dey,*

And by the agent Plenipotentiary of the United States of America,

> JOEL BARLOW.

Acknowledgments

———⟨∞⟩———

MY STORY IS A TRANSFORMATIONAL JOURNEY THAT HAS SPANNED
several continents, cultures, and religions. It elucidates the
challenges and the innate will of every human being to make
sense of and find purpose in his or her own life.

I am fortunate and deeply grateful to my wife, Barbara,
who has been with me for every step of my transformation
and has encouraged and prodded me for over twenty years
to tell my story in this book. I deeply love and adore my
daughter, Jessica, and my son, Jason, and I am thankful to
both for allowing and trusting me to share our family story.

I am grateful to my community at Temple Beth Am in Los
Angeles and to Rabbi Adam Kligfeld, our energetic, supportive, wise, and well-versed senior rabbi. They have afforded
me a safe place to worship, learn, and grow spiritually, and
to form deep and meaningful friendships.

It is a blessing and an honor to have a friend like Sharon
Dunas, co-president, NAMI Westside Los Angeles (namila.
org), who has tirelessly supported and counseled my family
to wellness during difficult moments of despair. I am also
grateful to our many friends at NAMI Support Groups,
NAMI Family-to-Family Classes, and InsightLA Meditation
Center, who have shared their stories and have helped me
to normalize my fear and anxiety.

I am very thankful to the very capable multilinguist
Henry Wudl, assistant Judaica librarian at Hebrew Union
College–Jewish Institute of Religion in Los Angeles, for
introducing me to the ancient and rich body of Judeo-Arabic
literature, written in Hebrew script for Jews in Arab lands.

I am deeply grateful to my friend Tom Fields-Meyer for his unsurpassed gift of listening with compassion and sensitivity. He is extraordinarily talented and gifted and I truly feel blessed to have had him guide me in telling my story.

I am delighted and immensely grateful to my wife, Barbara, for her amazing cover art, author's photo, map design, and for lending her care and artistic talents throughout the book. Barbara is a very gifted artist and has patiently taught me, as she has our children, how to appreciate art and music and how to incorporate them as integral parts of our lives, both inside and outside of our home.

My deep gratitude and appreciation also go to my in-laws, Bob and Ellen Levin, who accepted me as part of their family with unconditional love and have been very generous on many levels to my family and me.

Finally, I thank the exceptional and wonderful team at Luminare Press: Claire Flint Last, for her careful and thoughtful layout and design; and Patricia Marshall and Kim Harper-Kennedy for editing and overseeing the process to completion. I am grateful for their support and helpful suggestions.

About the Author

ED ELHADERI WAS BORN IN 1951 IN A NOMADIC VILLAGE IN THE Libyan Sahara. He graduated from the University of Tripoli at the top of his class, earning the First National Honor Award in engineering. He has a master's in chemical engineering from the University of Wisconsin-Madison and a Ph.D. in the same subject from the University of Southern California. A real estate broker and investor, he is active in his synagogue, a practitioner of mindful Buddhist meditation, and a teacher for the National Alliance on Mental Illness's Family to Family program. He lives in Los Angeles with his wife, Barbara. They are the proud parents of Jessica and Jason.